KT-423-292

THE HUGE BOOK OF HELL

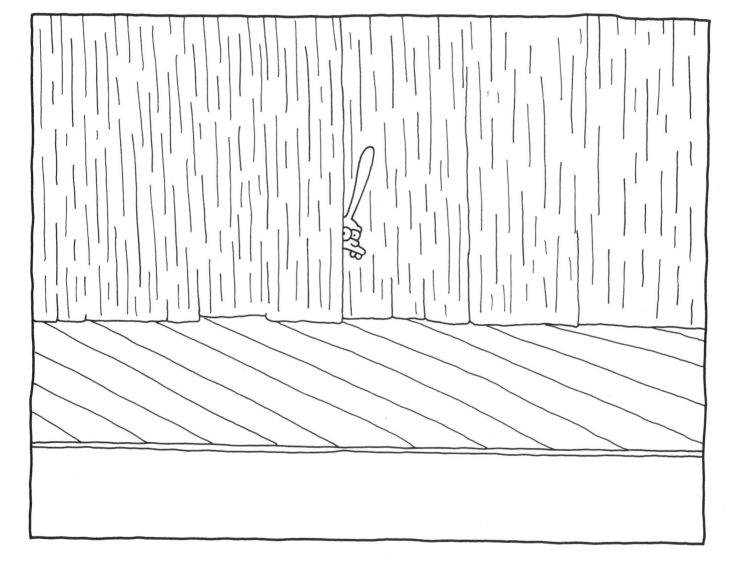

BY MATT GROENING

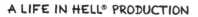

A LIFE IN HELL® PRODUCTION

OTHER "HELL" BOOKS BY YOUR CARTOON CHUM

AKBAR & JEFF'S GUIDE TO LIFE
BINKY'S GUIDE TO LOVE
CHILDHOOD IS HELL
HOW TO GO TO HELL
LOVE IS HELL
SCHOOL IS HELL
THE BIG BOOK OF HELL
THE ROAD TO HELL
WORK IS HELL

WORKS IN PROGRESS

SEVERAL MORE CARTOON BOOKS EVERY YEAR OR TWO
TILL I RUN OUT OF STEAM

HARPERCOLLINSPUBLISHERS
77-85 FULHAM PALACE ROAD,
HAMMERSMITH, LONDON W6 8JB
WWW.HARPERCOLLINS.CO.UK

THIS EDITION FIRST PUBLISHED 2005
1 3 5 7 9 8 6 4 2

ORIGINALLY PUBLISHED IN 1997 BY PENGUIN BOOKS.

COPYRIGHT © 1997, 2005 BY MATT GROENING PRODUCTIONS, INC.

ALL RIGHTS RESERVED UNDER INTERNATIONAL AND PAN AMERICAN COPYRIGHT CONVENTIONS.
NO PART OF THIS BOOK MAY BE USED OR REPRODUCED IN ANY MANNER
WHATSOEVER WITHOUT WRITTEN PERMISSION.

ISBN 0 00 719166 9

PRINTED AND BOUND IN BELGIUM BY PROOST NV, TURNHOUT

CONTENTS

DREAMLAND

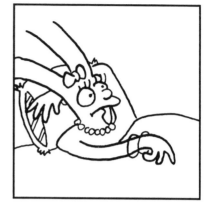

CREATIVE JUICES

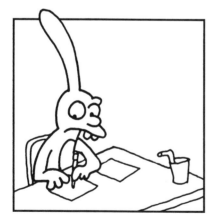

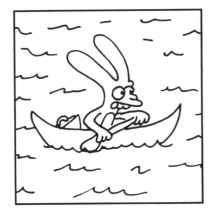

THE LAW OF THE BRINY DEEP

LIFE'S LITTLE BURDENS

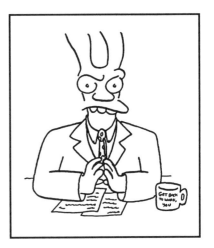

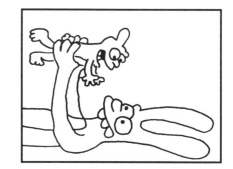

PARLOR TRICKS

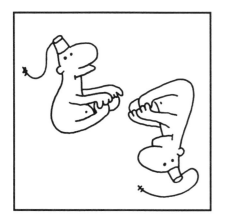

PARLOR TRICKS

SOUP DU JOUR

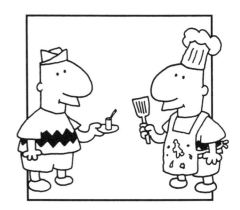

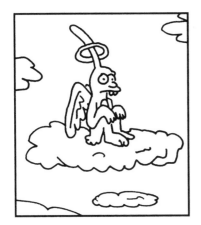

THE BIG PICTURE

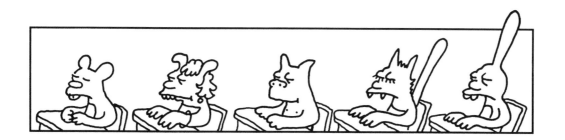

THE LEARNING EXPERIENCE

ENLIGHTENMENT IS HELL

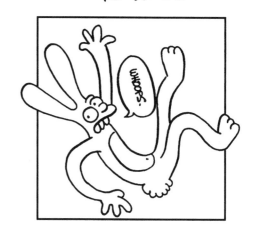

LET'S DANCE

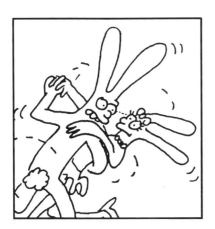

HAPPILY EVER AFTER

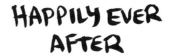

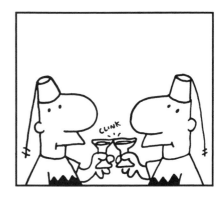

DREAMLAND

LIFE IN HELL
©1995 BY MATT GROENING
DO YOU EVER FANTASIZE ABOUT OTHER PEOPLE WHEN WE'RE MAKING LOVE?
NO, NOT REALLY.
ME NEITHER.

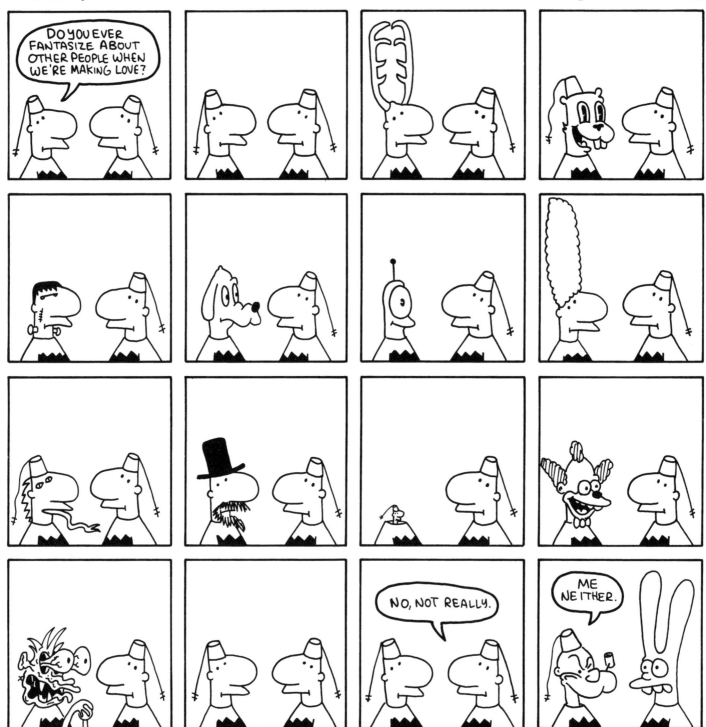

LIFE IN HELL
©1994 BY MATT GROENING
WILL AND ABE IN
KING OF MONSTER ISLAND
DAD! WE'RE HAVING THE FINAL BATTLE TO SEE WHO IS KING OF MONSTER ISLAND!
THIS MONSTER IS... GHOUL DIECLOPS!
THIS MONSTER IS... MEGA-VIRUS ZOMBIE!
THIS MONSTER IS... MONSTER ZERO FROM THE PLANET ZERO!
THIS MONSTER IS... ZEE GHOULER!
THIS MONSTER IS... IS...
IS... IS...
...TINA.
TINA?! YOU CAN'T HAVE A MONSTER NAMED TINA!!!
YES I DO.
NO!!!
TINA.
NO!!
TINA!
NO!!!
NO!!
TINA!
NO!
NO!!
NO!!
TINA!
I'M NOT PLAYING THIS GAME WITH YOU! YOU DON'T EVEN KNOW HOW TO PLAY IT RIGHT!
TINA IS KING OF MONSTER ISLAND.

LIFE IN HELL
©1993 BY MATT GROENING
LET'S SHARE OUR SECRET FANTASIES.
I COULD HUG YOU.
I COULD KISS YOU.
I COULD FONDLE YOU TILL YOU BEG FOR MERCY.
I COULD SQUEEZE YOU SO HARD YOUR EYES WOULD BULGE.
I COULD CARESS YOU TILL YOUR BRAIN FELL OUT.
I COULD STRANGLE YOU IN YOUR SLEEP.
I COULD FLING YOU OFF A CLIFF.
I COULD FEED YOU TO THE SHARKS.
I COULD POISON YOUR CEREAL.
I COULD BASH YOUR HEAD IN WITH A SLEDGEHAMMER.
I COULD GET A TRAINED DOBERMAN TO BITE YOUR FACE OFF.
I COULD SPEND THE REST OF MY LIFE MAKING BOTH OF US MISERABLE WITH LOW-LEVEL WHINING AND HOSTILITY.
I COULD SPEND THE REST OF MY LIFE MAKING BOTH OF US MISERABLE WITH JOYLESS SULKING AND SEXUAL ALIENATION.
THANK GOD THESE ARE ONLY FANTASIES.

LIFE IN HELL
©1987 BY MATT GROENING
OK, SO THEY LIVED HAPPILY EVER AFTER. THEN WHAT HAPPENED?
HOW CAN ANYONE EAT SOMETHING CALLED RUMP ROAST?
DO ANIMAL CRACKERS FEEL PAIN WHEN YOU BITE THEIR HEADS OFF?
WHY DO FLIES LAND ON DOG MANURE? DON'T THEY KNOW IT'S DOG MANURE?
HOW DO DEAD PEOPLE GET OUT OF THEIR GRAVES? DO THEY DIG TUNNELS?
WHEN IT COMES TO PEANUT BUTTER, DOES GOD PREFER CREAMY OR CHUNK-STYLE?
IS IT POSSIBLE TO HAVE SO MANY QUESTIONS FLYING AROUND INSIDE YOUR BRAIN THAT YOU CAN NEVER GO TO SLEEP AND EVENTUALLY YOU GO INSANE?
ZZZZ

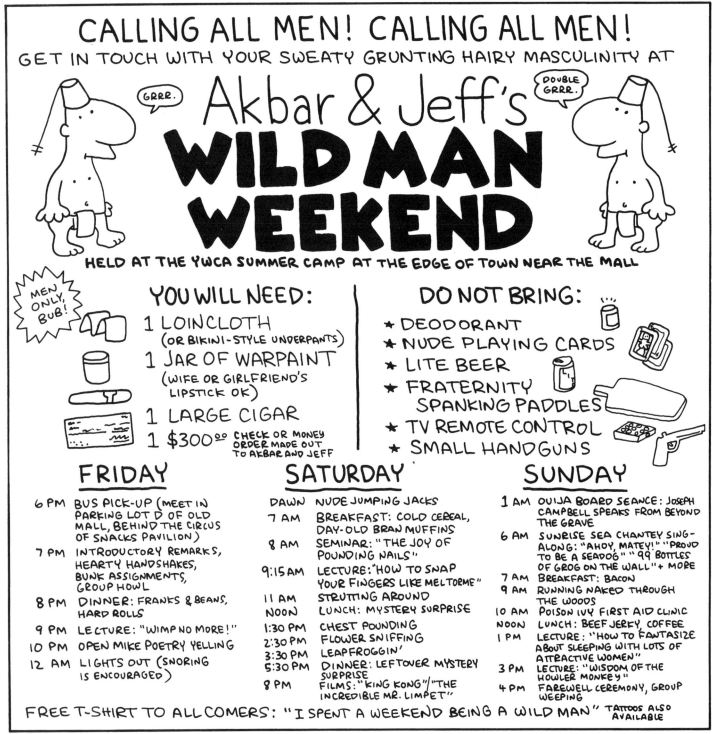

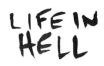
LIFE IN HELL

©1991 BY MATT GROENING

CALLING ALL MEN! CALLING ALL MEN!

GET IN TOUCH WITH YOUR SWEATY GRUNTING HAIRY MASCULINITY AT

GRRR.

DOUBLE GRRR.

Akbar & Jeff's
WILD MAN WEEKEND

HELD AT THE YWCA SUMMER CAMP AT THE EDGE OF TOWN NEAR THE MALL

MEN ONLY, BUB!

YOU WILL NEED:

1 LOINCLOTH (OR BIKINI-STYLE UNDERPANTS)

1 JAR OF WARPAINT (WIFE OR GIRLFRIEND'S LIPSTICK OK)

1 LARGE CIGAR

1 $300⁰⁰ CHECK OR MONEY ORDER MADE OUT TO AKBAR AND JEFF

DO NOT BRING:

★ DEODORANT
★ NUDE PLAYING CARDS
★ LITE BEER
★ FRATERNITY SPANKING PADDLES
★ TV REMOTE CONTROL
★ SMALL HANDGUNS

FRIDAY

6 PM BUS PICK-UP (MEET IN PARKING LOT D OF OLD MALL, BEHIND THE CIRCUS OF SNACKS PAVILION)

7 PM INTRODUCTORY REMARKS, HEARTY HANDSHAKES, BUNK ASSIGNMENTS, GROUP HOWL

8 PM DINNER: FRANKS & BEANS, HARD ROLLS

9 PM LECTURE: "WIMP NO MORE!"

10 PM OPEN MIKE POETRY YELLING

12 AM LIGHTS OUT (SNORING IS ENCOURAGED)

SATURDAY

DAWN NUDE JUMPING JACKS

7 AM BREAKFAST: COLD CEREAL, DAY-OLD BRAN MUFFINS

8 AM SEMINAR: "THE JOY OF POUNDING NAILS"

9:15AM LECTURE:"HOW TO SNAP YOUR FINGERS LIKE MEL TORME"

11 AM STRUTTING AROUND

NOON LUNCH: MYSTERY SURPRISE

1:30 PM CHEST POUNDING

2:30 PM FLOWER SNIFFING

3:30 PM LEAPFROGGIN'

5:30 PM DINNER: LEFTOVER MYSTERY SURPRISE

8 PM FILMS: "KING KONG"/"THE INCREDIBLE MR. LIMPET"

SUNDAY

1 AM OUIJA BOARD SEANCE: JOSEPH CAMPBELL SPEAKS FROM BEYOND THE GRAVE

6 AM SUNRISE SEA CHANTEY SING-ALONG: "AHOY, MATEY!" "PROUD TO BE A SEADOG" "99 BOTTLES OF GROG ON THE WALL"+ MORE

7 AM BREAKFAST: BACON

9 AM RUNNING NAKED THROUGH THE WOODS

10 AM POISON IVY FIRST AID CLINIC

NOON LUNCH: BEEF JERKY, COFFEE

1 PM LECTURE: "HOW TO FANTASIZE ABOUT SLEEPING WITH LOTS OF ATTRACTIVE WOMEN"

3 PM LECTURE: "WISDOM OF THE HOWLER MONKEY"

4 PM FAREWELL CEREMONY, GROUP WEEPING

FREE T-SHIRT TO ALL COMERS: "I SPENT A WEEKEND BEING A WILD MAN" TATTOOS ALSO AVAILABLE

©1993 BY MATT GROENING

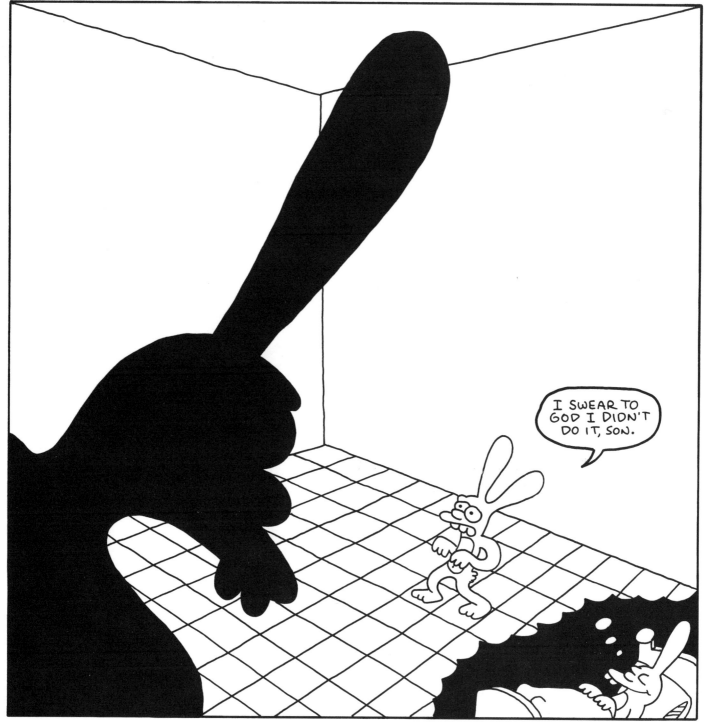

I SWEAR TO GOD I DIDN'T DO IT, SON.

LIFE IN HELL
©1994 BY MATT GROENING
INTERVIEW WITH A 3-YEAR-OLD VAMPIRE
STARRING ABE
ARE YOU A VAMPIRE?
YEAH.
WHY DO YOU WEAR A CAPE?
I'M DRACUYA!
DOES YOUR CAPE GIVE YOU SPECIAL POWERS?
IT GOTS RED ON THE BACK AND BYACK ON THE FRONT.
WHAT DO YOU LIKE TO DO?
SUCK BYUD!
WHY?
BECAUSE I'M VERY THIRSTY.
WHAT ELSE DO YOU LIKE TO DO?
FYI TO MY CASTLE.
WHAT DO YOU DO THERE?
SUCK BYUD AGAIN.
ARE THERE BABY VAMPIRES?
OF COURSE.
WHAT DO THEY DO?
SUCK BYUD FROM A BOTTLE.
DO VAMPIRES EAT COUNT CHOCULA CEREAL?
VAMPIRES JUST SUCK BYUD, DAD.
WHERE DO YOU SLEEP?
IN A COFFIN.
IS YOUR COFFIN YOUR BEDROOM?
NO, MY COFFIN IS MY BED.
IS IT COMFY IN YOUR COFFIN?
NO MORE QUESTIONS, DAD.
WHY DON'T YOU LIKE THE DAYTIME?
NO MORE QUESTIONS, DAD.
JUST ONE MORE--
I FYI AWAY, BEARDFACE!

CREATIVE JUICES

WHAT DO YOU LIKE TO DO?
SUCK BYUD!

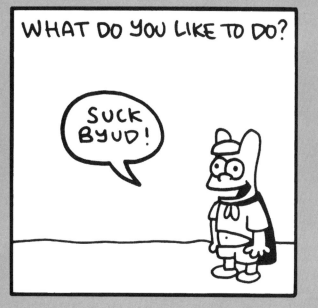

LIFE IN HELL
©1994 BY MATT GROENING
HEY KIDS!
LET'S DRAW MONSTERS
I GOT A BETTER IDEA, MATT. I'LL TELL YOU WHAT TO DRAW AND YOU DRAW WHAT I TELL YOU TO DRAW.
THIS IS CLAW, THE BLOOD MONSTER!
HIS UGLY FORM HAS SEVEN EYES, BLOOD DRIPPIN' DOWN HIS TEETH, AND A FLOWER HEAD, AND A LONG TAIL, AND HE HAS VAMP FANGS, AND HE BLOWS FIRE. THE BLOOD MONSTER IS ONE OF THE STRONGEST HUMAN-BODY MONSTERS IN THE WORLD.
NOW IT'S TIME TO DRAW THE HALF-HUMAN, HALF-MONSTER!
HE'S HALF HUMAN AND HALF MONSTER. HE HAS ONE HUMAN EAR AND A LITTLE HEAD. HE COULD SPIT FIRE FROM EACH OF ITS MOUTHS. HE COULD TURN PEOPLE INTO ROCKS. HE'S TRICKY BECAUSE HE CAN GO UNDERGROUND EVERYWHERE — AUSTRALIA, TURKEY, CHINA, JAMBOOTA. [WHAT'S JAMBOOTA?] JAMBOOTA HAS LOTS OF APES.
MY BRAIN IS GETTING AN IDEA! KI-JOO, THE JAPANESE MONSTER!
HE HAS A HUNDRED HEADS AND A HUNDRED ARMS AND HE COULD SWITCH HIS BODY AROUND. [TRY AGAIN. I CAN'T DRAW THAT MANY HEADS AND ARMS.] OK. HE HAS ONE LITTLE HEAD, AND A TAIL, AND TWO THINGS ON HIS TAIL, AND HE COULD KICK EVERYWHERE IN THE UNIVERSE. HE COULD KICK THE STARS AND THE WORLD. HE COULD KICK THE MOON.
I WANT A TURN! THIS IS GROVER, THE PUPPY-DOG!
HE'S LITTLE AND NICE LITTLE PUPPY-DOG. AND HE GOT BIG CLAWS AND FAT EYES. AND HE GOTS A FAT TUMMY AND AND A TAIL.
THAT'S NOT A MONSTER, ABE.
YES HE IS. HE GOTS BLOOD ON HIS TEETH.

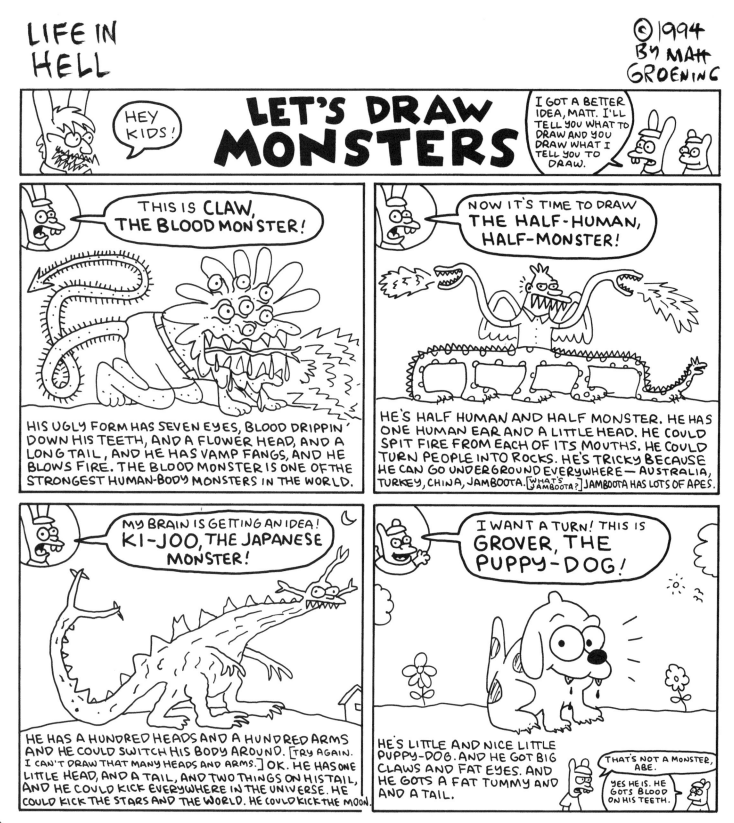

LIFE IN HELL
©1991 BY MATT GROENING
WITH HELP FROM MILI SMYTHE, BARBARA McADAMS, PETER ALEXANDER, & LISA PINEBIRD
AKBAR & JEFF'S HAIRDOS AROUND THE WORLD
"THE COQUETTE"
"THE NATTY DREADLOCKS"
"THE INFANT"
"THE REBEL WITHOUT A CAUSE"
"THE RINGO"
"THE PERMA-PARTY HAT"
"THE DEBBIE"
"THE NUCLEAR HOLOCAUST"
"THE GEISHA"
"THE LARRY OF THE 3 STOOGES"
"THE SPROUTING HAIR PLUG IMPLANTS"
"THE SMURF"
"THE MARGE SIMPSON"
"THE NOT-QUITE-DONE YET"
"THE MAN OF THE '80s, I MEAN '90s"
"PERFECTION"

LIFE IN HELL

IS BEING POLITICALLY CORRECT REALLY THAT IMPORTANT TO YOU?

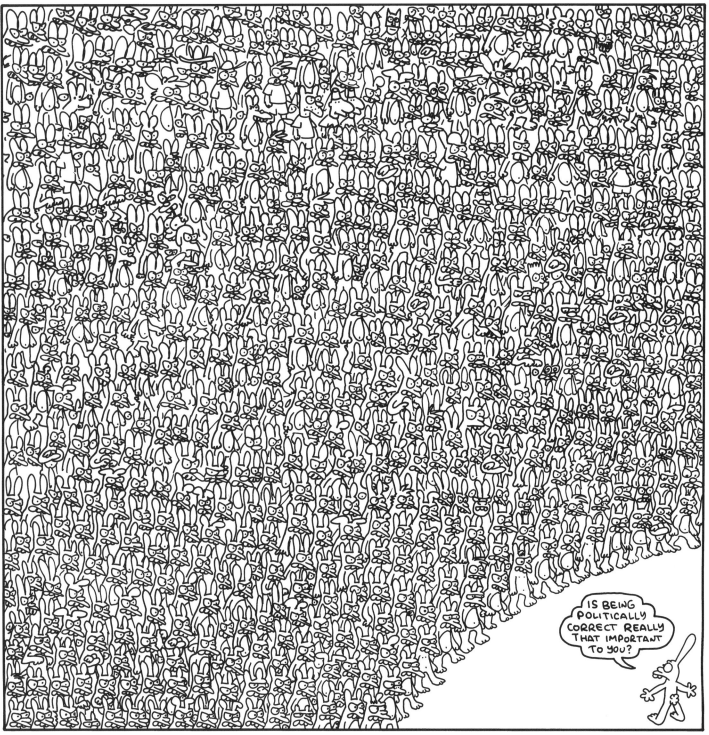

LIFE IN HELL

© 1994 BY MATT GROENING

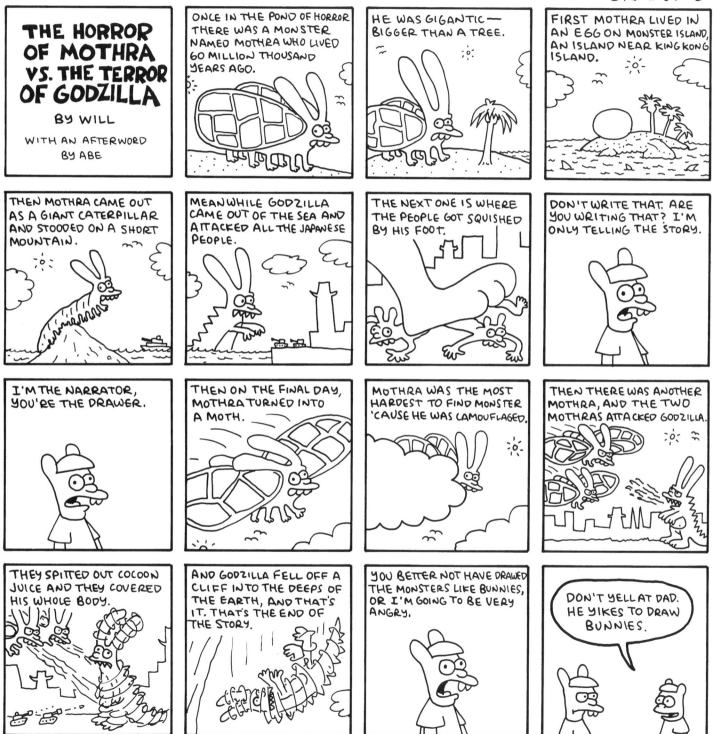

THE HORROR OF MOTHRA VS. THE TERROR OF GODZILLA

BY WILL

WITH AN AFTERWORD BY ABE

ONCE IN THE POND OF HORROR THERE WAS A MONSTER NAMED MOTHRA WHO LIVED 60 MILLION THOUSAND YEARS AGO.

HE WAS GIGANTIC — BIGGER THAN A TREE.

FIRST MOTHRA LIVED IN AN EGG ON MONSTER ISLAND, AN ISLAND NEAR KING KONG ISLAND.

THEN MOTHRA CAME OUT AS A GIANT CATERPILLAR AND STOODED ON A SHORT MOUNTAIN.

MEANWHILE GODZILLA CAME OUT OF THE SEA AND ATTACKED ALL THE JAPANESE PEOPLE.

THE NEXT ONE IS WHERE THE PEOPLE GOT SQUISHED BY HIS FOOT.

DON'T WRITE THAT. ARE YOU WRITING THAT? I'M ONLY TELLING THE STORY.

I'M THE NARRATOR, YOU'RE THE DRAWER.

THEN ON THE FINAL DAY, MOTHRA TURNED INTO A MOTH.

MOTHRA WAS THE MOST HARDEST TO FIND MONSTER 'CAUSE HE WAS CAMOUFLAGED.

THEN THERE WAS ANOTHER MOTHRA, AND THE TWO MOTHRAS ATTACKED GODZILLA.

THEY SPITTED OUT COCOON JUICE AND THEY COVERED HIS WHOLE BODY.

AND GODZILLA FELL OFF A CLIFF INTO THE DEEPS OF THE EARTH, AND THAT'S IT. THAT'S THE END OF THE STORY.

YOU BETTER NOT HAVE DRAWED THE MONSTERS LIKE BUNNIES, OR I'M GOING TO BE VERY ANGRY.

DON'T YELL AT DAD. HE YIKES TO DRAW BUNNIES.

13

©1990 BY MATT GROENING WITH LYNDA BARRY

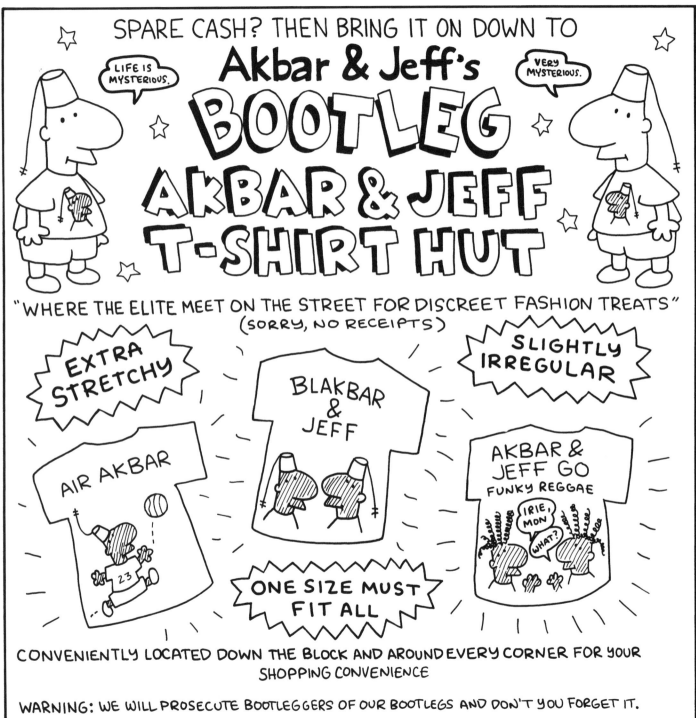

LIFE IN HELL

©1990 BY MATT GROENING

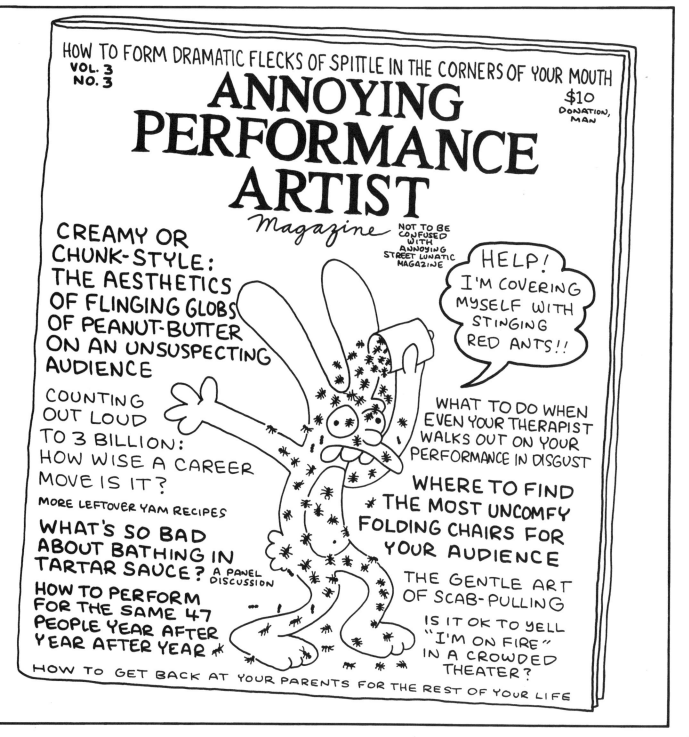

MANY WOULD-BE YOUNG ARTISTS WRITE TO LIFE IN HELL HEADQUARTERS ASKING, "HOW CAN I LEARN TO DRAW LIKE A PRO? HOW CAN I MASTER THE CRAFT, THE PRECISION, AND THE STEADY HAND REQUIRED TO CREATE ART OF DISTINCTION AND LASTING WORTH?" BEATS ME. BUT IF YOU'RE CONTENT WITH DRAWING A CRUDE BUT CUDDLY CARTOON CREATURE OVER AND OVER AGAIN, THEN SIT UP STRAIGHT, PUT ON A LOOSE SMOCK, AND PAY ATTENTION. HERE'S

HOW TO DRAW BINKY

© 1981 BY MATT GROENING

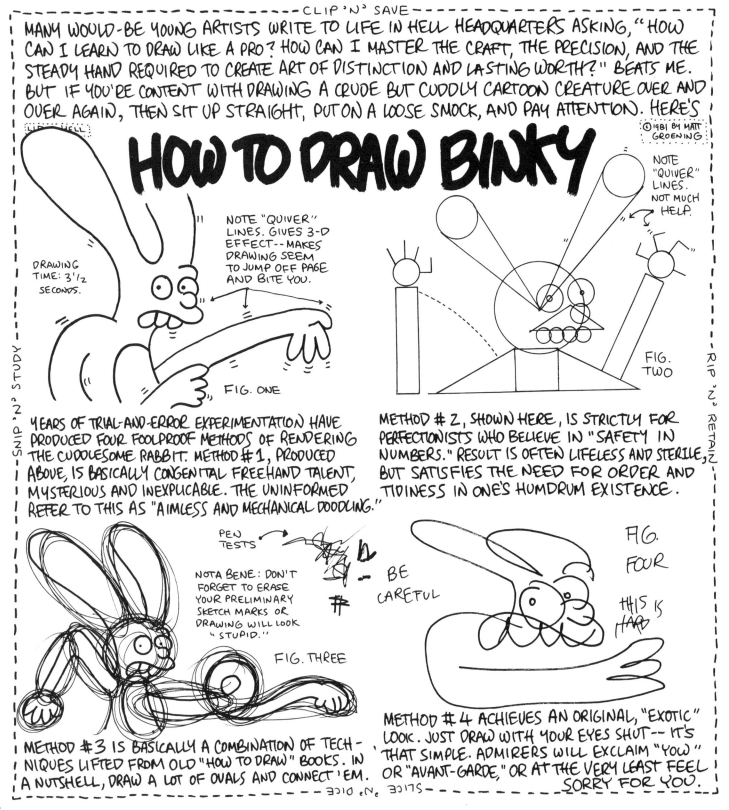

DRAWING TIME: 3½ SECONDS.

NOTE "QUIVER" LINES. GIVES 3-D EFFECT-- MAKES DRAWING SEEM TO JUMP OFF PAGE AND BITE YOU.

FIG. ONE

NOTE "QUIVER" LINES. NOT MUCH HELP.

FIG. TWO

4 YEARS OF TRIAL-AND-ERROR EXPERIMENTATION HAVE PRODUCED FOUR FOOLPROOF METHODS OF RENDERING THE CUDDLESOME RABBIT. METHOD #1, PRODUCED ABOVE, IS BASICALLY CONGENITAL FREEHAND TALENT, MYSTERIOUS AND INEXPLICABLE. THE UNINFORMED REFER TO THIS AS "AIMLESS AND MECHANICAL DOODLING."

METHOD #2, SHOWN HERE, IS STRICTLY FOR PERFECTIONISTS WHO BELIEVE IN "SAFETY IN NUMBERS." RESULT IS OFTEN LIFELESS AND STERILE, BUT SATISFIES THE NEED FOR ORDER AND TIDINESS IN ONE'S HUMDRUM EXISTENCE.

PEN TESTS

NOTA BENE: DON'T FORGET TO ERASE YOUR PRELIMINARY SKETCH MARKS OR DRAWING WILL LOOK "STUPID."

BE CAREFUL

FIG. THREE

FIG. FOUR

THIS IS HARD

METHOD #3 IS BASICALLY A COMBINATION OF TECH-NIQUES LIFTED FROM OLD "HOW TO DRAW" BOOKS. IN A NUTSHELL, DRAW A LOT OF OVALS AND CONNECT 'EM.

METHOD #4 ACHIEVES AN ORIGINAL, "EXOTIC" LOOK. JUST DRAW WITH YOUR EYES SHUT-- IT'S THAT SIMPLE. ADMIRERS WILL EXCLAIM "YOW" OR "AVANT-GARDE," OR AT THE VERY LEAST FEEL SORRY FOR YOU.

© 1986 BY MATT GROENING WITH GARY PANTER

LIFE IN HELL
DRAWN WHILE SICK

HOW TO BE AN ARTIST IN TORMENT

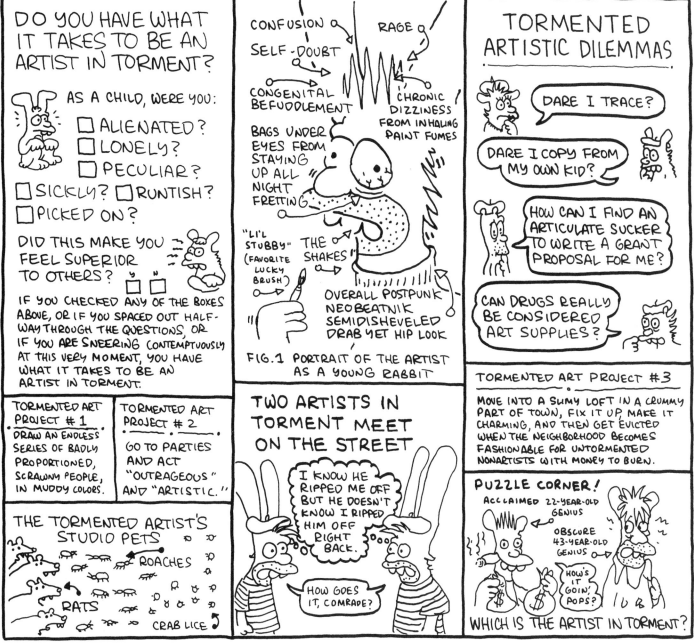

DO YOU HAVE WHAT IT TAKES TO BE AN ARTIST IN TORMENT?

AS A CHILD, WERE YOU:
- ☐ ALIENATED?
- ☐ LONELY?
- ☐ PECULIAR?
- ☐ SICKLY? ☐ RUNTISH?
- ☐ PICKED ON?

DID THIS MAKE YOU FEEL SUPERIOR TO OTHERS? ☐ ☐

IF YOU CHECKED ANY OF THE BOXES ABOVE, OR IF YOU SPACED OUT HALF-WAY THROUGH THE QUESTIONS, OR IF YOU ARE SNEERING CONTEMPTUOUSLY AT THIS VERY MOMENT, YOU HAVE WHAT IT TAKES TO BE AN ARTIST IN TORMENT.

TORMENTED ART PROJECT # 1
DRAW AN ENDLESS SERIES OF BADLY PROPORTIONED, SCRAWNY PEOPLE, IN MUDDY COLORS.

TORMENTED ART PROJECT # 2
GO TO PARTIES AND ACT "OUTRAGEOUS" AND "ARTISTIC."

THE TORMENTED ARTIST'S STUDIO PETS
ROACHES
RATS
CRAB LICE

CONFUSION
SELF-DOUBT
RAGE
CONGENITAL BEFUDDLEMENT
CHRONIC DIZZINESS FROM INHALING PAINT FUMES
BAGS UNDER EYES FROM STAYING UP ALL NIGHT FRETTING
"LI'L STUBBY" (FAVORITE LUCKY BRUSH)
THE "SHAKES"
OVERALL POSTPUNK NEOBEATNIK SEMIDISHEVELED DRAB YET HIP LOOK

FIG. 1 PORTRAIT OF THE ARTIST AS A YOUNG RABBIT

TWO ARTISTS IN TORMENT MEET ON THE STREET

I KNOW HE RIPPED ME OFF BUT HE DOESN'T KNOW I RIPPED HIM OFF RIGHT BACK.

HOW GOES IT, COMRADE?

TORMENTED ARTISTIC DILEMMAS

DARE I TRACE?

DARE I COPY FROM MY OWN KID?

HOW CAN I FIND AN ARTICULATE SUCKER TO WRITE A GRANT PROPOSAL FOR ME?

CAN DRUGS REALLY BE CONSIDERED ART SUPPLIES?

TORMENTED ART PROJECT #3
MOVE INTO A SLIMY LOFT IN A CRUMMY PART OF TOWN, FIX IT UP, MAKE IT CHARMING, AND THEN GET EVICTED WHEN THE NEIGHBORHOOD BECOMES FASHIONABLE FOR UNTORMENTED NONARTISTS WITH MONEY TO BURN.

PUZZLE CORNER!
ACCLAIMED 22-YEAR-OLD GENIUS
OBSCURE 43-YEAR-OLD GENIUS
HOW'S IT GOIN', POPS?
WHICH IS THE ARTIST IN TORMENT?

©1986 BY MATT GROENING

THE EVOLUTION OF MY CARTOON CAREER

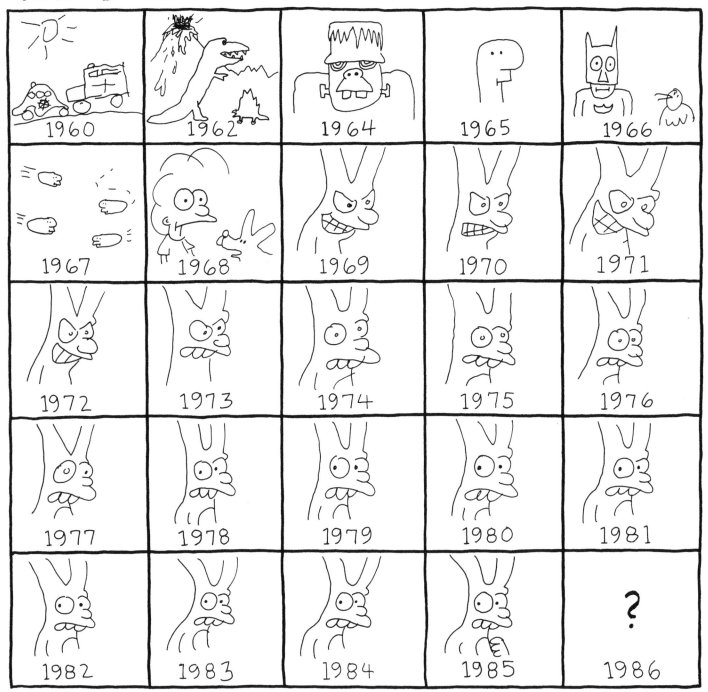

LIFE IN HELL
©1987 BY MATT GROENING
HOW TO AVERT YOUR GAZE FROM THE UNSIGHTLY POOR
YOUNG CODGER
NO. 1 "THE BEST IN DISGRUNTLEMENT" 1987 $3.95
THE LATEST ETIQUETTE RULES:
• SNIFFING SUSPICIOUSLY
• LAUGHING MIRTHLESSLY
• QUIBBLING FOR THE SHEER JOYLESSNESS OF IT
FRIGHTENING CRIME ANECDOTES FROM NEARBY NEIGHBORHOODS
LOOK AT THOSE JERKS OVER THERE--THEY THINK THEY'RE HAVING FUN.
STAYING HOME AND RAPIDLY SWITCHING TV CHANNELS ALL NIGHT WITH THE REMOTE CONTROL
HOW TO CHANGE YOUR HAIRDO WITHOUT CHANGING YOUR POLITICS
THE POOR DELUDED FOOLS.
TRANSCENDENTAL MASTICATION: ONE WAY TO MAKE MINISCULE PORTIONS SERVED AT FINE RESTAURANTS LAST FOR AN ENTIRE MEAL
THAT HORRIBLE CRAZY RAP MUSIC
THE TRAGEDY OF HAVING EXQUISITE TASTE: NOTHING IS EVER GOOD ENOUGH

BOX O' HELL
©1983 BY MATT GROENING
FULSOME FILMS IN ASSOCIATION WITH MAVERICKER MARKETING, INC. AND STUBCO®
PROUDLY PRESENT
SNOW WHITE
and the NEW
SEVEN DEADLY
DWARFS
IN VIBRATING "3-D" ANNOYORAMA®
INTRODUCING SHEBA JONES AS "SNOW"
CONSIDER THE MARKETING POSSIBILITIES.
"HUNKY"
"PUNKY"
"HERPY"
"TOOTSY"
"PESKY"
"COKEY"
"THE PSYCHOPATH"
ANOTHER BINKOTRONIX TAX WRITE-OFF
STARRING SEVERAL LOW-PAID UNCREDITED MIDGETS IN HOT RUBBER SUITS · MUSIC RIPPED OFF BY 'BO' RINGMUN "DWARF THEME (I'M COMING)" SUNG BY THE KISSIES
EXECUTIVE PRODUCER SOME GLORIFIED ACCOUNTANT/WRITTEN BY BINKY X, PAT HOBBY, AND VINCENT CAULFIELD/BASED ON A COMIC STRIP BY MATT GROENING
DIRECTED BY STINKY BARKLER/ FILMED IN GRAIN-O-VISION
DEMOGRAPHIC RESEARCH BY LOWEST COMMON DENOMINATOR INC./PRESOLD TO CABLE TV, SUCKERS
BARGAIN MATINEE TIL 1 P.M. ALL SOFT DRINKS ONLY $3
R RESTRICTED
LONG LINES, POOR PROJECTION, AND RUDE AUDIENCES MAY BE UNSUITABLE FOR SOME VIEWERS.

LIFE IN HELL
©1986 BY MATT GROENING
HOW TO DRAW BINKY THE EASY WAY
1. START WITH A CIRCLE, LIKE THIS.
2. THEN ADD THE FEATURES, AND ERASE THE BASIC GUIDELINES.
3. LO AND BEHOLD!
HOW TO DRAW BINKY THE EASIER WAY
1. FROM THE TIME YOU BEGIN GOING TO SCHOOL, DRAW WHENEVER THE TEACHER ISN'T LOOKING.
2. DEVELOP A SIMPLE CHARACTER AND DRAW IT OBSESSIVELY THOUSANDS AND THOUSANDS OF TIMES.
3. YEAH!!
HOW TO DRAW BINKY THE EASIEST WAY
1 CLOSE EYES
2. GO!!
3. VOILA!!!!

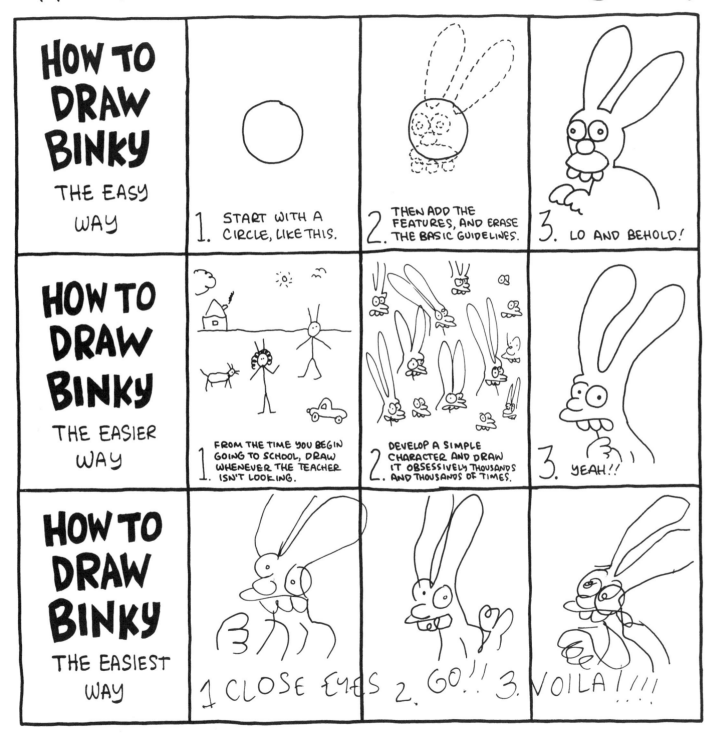

LIFE IN HELL

PAINT WHAT YOU FEEL, KIDS.

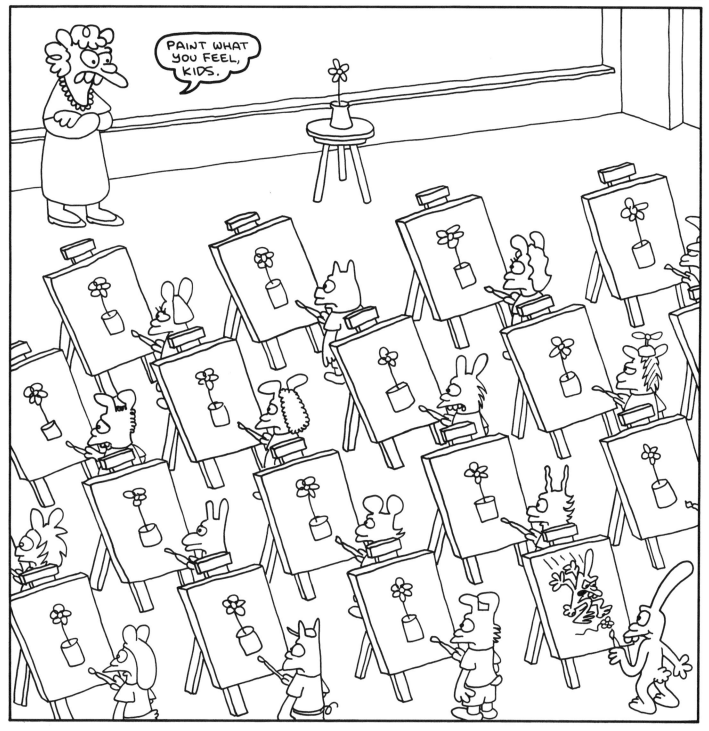

THE LAW OF THE BRINY DEEP

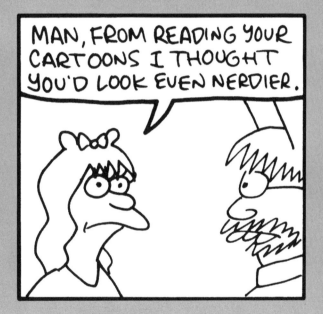

LIFE IN HELL

©1994 BY MATT GROENING

FANS WANT TO KNOW
IS SMITHERS GAY???
DO YOU GET A LIFETIME SUPPLY OF BUTTERFINGERS?
YOU SHOULD HAVE O.J. SIMPSON ON THE SHOW. YOU KNOW, CUZ HE'S A SIMPSON. GET IT?
I WROTE YOU THREE TIMES BUT YOU NEVER SENT ME A DRAWING OF MARGE SIMPSON NAKED.
NO ONE'S GONNA BELIEVE I'M TALKING TO THE GUY WHO CREATED THE SIMPSONS. MY WHOLE FAMILY HATES YOUR SHOW!!
MAN, FROM READING YOUR CARTOONS I THOUGHT YOU'D LOOK EVEN NERDIER.
THEY SAY ON THE INTERNET THAT YOU AND LYNDA BARRY LIVED IN A TEEPEE DURING COLLEGE. IS THAT TRUE??
IT WAS MORE OF A YURT, MAN.
IS GRAMPA SIMPSON GAY??
DO YOU GET ANY ROYALTIES FROM THOSE BOOTLEG BART SANCHEZ FIGURINES FROM TIJUANA?
FROM ALL THE HOOPLA YOU'D THINK IT WAS HOMER SIMPSON WHO MURDERED SOMEBODY!
DO YOU STILL DRAW EVERY FRAME OF THE SIMPSONS YOURSELF?
IS BART GAY??
IF YOU EVER NEED A NEW VOICE FOR HOMER, I'M YOUR MAN! I LOVE DONUTS! YES, MR. BURNS! DON'T HAVE A COW! I LOVE HOT DOGS! D'OHH!!
REMEMBER ABOUT FIVE YEARS AGO WHEN I GAVE YOU THE IDEA FOR THE SIMPSONS IN A BAR?
I'M YOUR BIGGEST FAN. I'VE GOT EVERYTHING YOU'VE EVER DONE. WHAT'S THAT THERE?
A LIFE IN HELL BOOK.
NEVER HEARD OF IT.

LIFE IN HELL

I PLEAD ABSOLUTELY 100% NOT GUILTY.

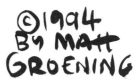

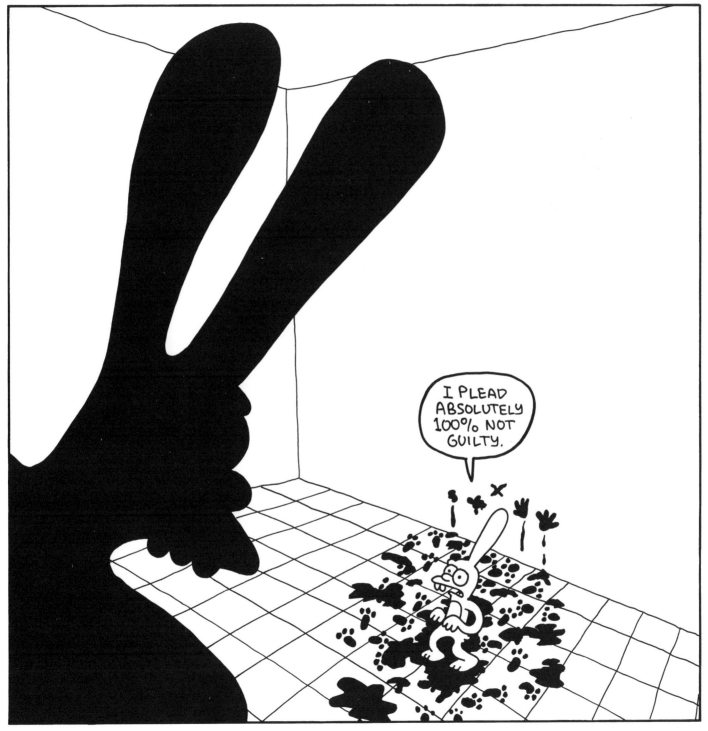

LIFE IN HELL
©1990 BY MATT GROENING
THE LAW OF THE BRINY DEEP
ANOTHER TRUE-LIFE NATURE ADVENTURE
ONE SUNNY AFTERNOON LAST SUMMER I WAS LYING IN MY HAMMOCK IN THE BACKYARD WHEN I HEARD SOME YELLING.
HEY UGLY!!
I PEEKED OVER THE FENCE AND SAW TWO KIDS STARING MALEVOLENTLY AT A SMALL TYKE.
THEY BEGAN TO TAUNT THE LITTLE GUY.
HOW'S IT GOING, DIAPER BABY?
I'M NOT A DIAPER BABY.
WHA'D YOU SAY?
SAID I'M NOT A DIAPER BABY.
ARE YOU CALLING US LIARS?
JUST THEN A BIG GUY SHOWED UP. HE TOWERED OVER THE LITTLE BULLIES.
WHAT'S THE PROBLEM HERE?
NO PROBLEM, MAN.
OH, I THINK THERE'S A PROBLEM, ALL RIGHT. AND YOU TWO ARE THE PROBLEM.
WE WASN'T DOIN' NUTHIN, MAN.
THE BIG GUY GLARED AT THE BULLIES FOR A MOMENT, THEN LUNGED AT THEM AND GRABBED THEIR BIKES.
HEY, MAN!
GIVE US BACK OUR BIKES, MAN!
THE BIG GUY JUST STOOD THERE WITH THE BIKES WHILE THE KIDS YELLED. THEN HE TURNED ON HIS HEELS AND WALKED OFF, CARRYING THE BIKES.
HEY, MAN!
OUR BIKES!!
THE BIG GUY MARCHED ONTO THE MIDDLE OF THE NEARBY FOOTBRIDGE, AND DANGLED THE BIKES OVER THE CANAL.
YOU BETTER NOT!!
KER-SPLOOSH!!
TEACH YOU TO PICK ON KIDS SMALLER THAN YOU.
THE LITTLE BULLIES RAN OFF, SWEARING. THE BIG GUY JUST LAUGHED AND WALKED AWAY.
WE'RE COMIN' BACK WITH OUR GANG AND WE'RE GONNA KILL YOU!
HA HA HA
WE'RE GONNA BURN YOUR HOUSE DOWN, MAN!
I WALKED OVER TO THE TOP OF THE FOOTBRIDGE AND STOOD THERE WITH SOME NEIGHBOR KIDS LOOKING AT THE BIKES SUBMERGED IN THE SHALLOW CANAL.
THEN THE LITTLE GUY WHO'D BEEN TEASED PIPED UP.
WELL, YOU KNOW THE LAW OF THE BRINY DEEP.
IF YOU CAN SALVAGE SOMETHING FROM THE OCEAN, IT'S YOURS.
THE NEIGHBOR KIDS WERE CONVINCED. THEY WADED INTO THE CANAL, PULLED OUT THE BIKES, AND SPED OFF, WHOOPING. THE LITTLE GUY AND I STOOD THERE, WATCHING.
LAW OF THE BRINY DEEP!!
YEE-HAW!
I TURNED AROUND TO TALK TO THE LITTLE GUY, BUT HE WAS ALREADY HALF A BLOCK AWAY, RUNNING LIKE HELL.

LIFE IN HELL

©1989 BY MATT GROENING

I THINK THE JURY BOUGHT OUR ALIBI.

LIFE IN HELL
©1996 BY MATT GROENING
WILL & ABE DISCUSS THE PROBLEMS OF OUR TIME
TODAY'S TOPIC: VIOLENCE
I THINK PEOPLE WHO LIKE VIOLENCE LIKE IT BECAUSE THEY LIKE TO IMAGINE THE PAIN.
AND PEOPLE WHO DON'T LIKE VIOLENCE DON'T LIKE IT 'CAUSE IT'S GROSS. AND THEY DON'T LIKE TO IMAGINE HOW PAINFUL IT IS.
THERE'S THREE MAIN KINDS OF BAD VIOLENCE.
THERE'S THE KNIFE. WHEN YOU SEE A KNIFE IN A KNIFE MOVIE YOU COULD SEE IT CHOP OFF A HEAD.
OR ANY OTHER PARTS OF THE BODY.
THE SECOND KIND OF BAD VIOLENCE IS THE GUN. IT JUST MEANS A LOT OF PEOPLE GET SHOT. YOU DON'T SEE ANY BLOOD AT ALL, USUALLY.
THE THIRD KIND OF BAD VIOLENCE IS EXPLOSIONS. THEY'RE THE LEAST DISGUSTING. YOU DON'T SEE ANYONE EXPLODE -- YOU JUST SEE THE WHOLE BUILDING EXPLODE.
THE GOOD KIND OF VIOLENCE IS CARTOONS.
YEAH!
IN CARTOON VIOLENCE NOBODY DIES. BECAUSE IF THEY DID DIE THE SHOW WOULD BE OVER AND PEOPLE WOULD START LOSING INTEREST.
THERE'S A LOT OF SCREAMING, SOUND EFFECTS, AND A WHOLE BUNCH OF MUSIC. YOU SEE A LOT OF DYNAMITE IN CARTOONS. BUT THEY DON'T DIE BECAUSE THE ARTISTS WANT TO GO ON AND ON. IN BUGS BUNNY, PEOPLE SOMETIMES GET EXPLODED BUT THEIR FACES JUST TURN BLACK.
THERE'S ALSO POKING IN THE EYE WITH THE TWO FRONT FINGERS. THIS HAPPENS IN THE THREE STOOGES, TOM & JERRY, AND THE "TOY STORY" CD-ROM.
THE KIND OF VIOLENCE I DON'T LIKE IS WHEN THEY STICK A KNIFE IN YOUR HEART AND THEY PULL OUT THE KNIFE AND YOUR HEART IS ON THE MIDDLE OF THE KNIFE.
AND THEY HOLD IT UP AND GO "YAW!!!"
SO SHOULD THERE BE MORE VIOLENCE OR LESS VIOLENCE?
A LITTLE BIT MORE VIOLENCE.

BAD KID
THE MAGAZINE FOR TODAY'S NORMAL AVERAGE HYPERACTIVE UNDERACHIEVING NASTY UNGRATEFUL SPOILED LITTLE SMARTASS
FALL 1983 25¢
DON'T NEED NO GODDAMN APPROVAL
THEY'RE BIG BUT CLUMSY
THE FINE ART OF OUTRUNNING ADULTS
L'IL STINKER
HOW CUTE TODDLERS' T-SHIRTS CAN MARK US FOR LIFE
ADVANCED COVERT SIBLING RIVALRY
DIPPING THEIR TOOTHBRUSHES IN THE TOILET WHEN NOBODY'S LOOKING
HOW TO LAUGH KNOWINGLY AT DIRTY JOKES YOU DON'T UNDERSTAND
THE ADVANTAGES OF HAVING ALCOHOLIC PARENTS
THEY DON'T NOTICE DETAILS
"WHERE'S MIKE HUNT?" AND OTHER WAYS TO DRIVE SUBSTITUTE TEACHERS OUT OF THEIR MINDS
I'M SORRY, SIR. TESTS SHOW THIS BOY IS DEEPLY AUTISTIC.
WOW-- ME ARTISTIC?
TWISTING, TWITCHING, and TAPPING
THREE WAYS TO PASS TIME AT YOUR SCHOOLDESK
LET'S BE DOUBLY ANNOYING
MISSPELL THE OBSCENITIES WHEN WE SPRAYPAINT 'EM
PICKING UP FUTURE BEHAVIOR TIPS FROM YOUR PARENTS' SCREAMING ARGUMENTS
EXISTENTIAL INCORRIGIBILITY: ONE YOUTH'S JUSTIFICATION FOR THROWING TANTRUMS IN RESTAURANTS
ARE ALL ADULTS BIG FAT LIARS?

LIFE IN HELL

IF IT DOESN'T FIT, YOU MUST ACQUIT.

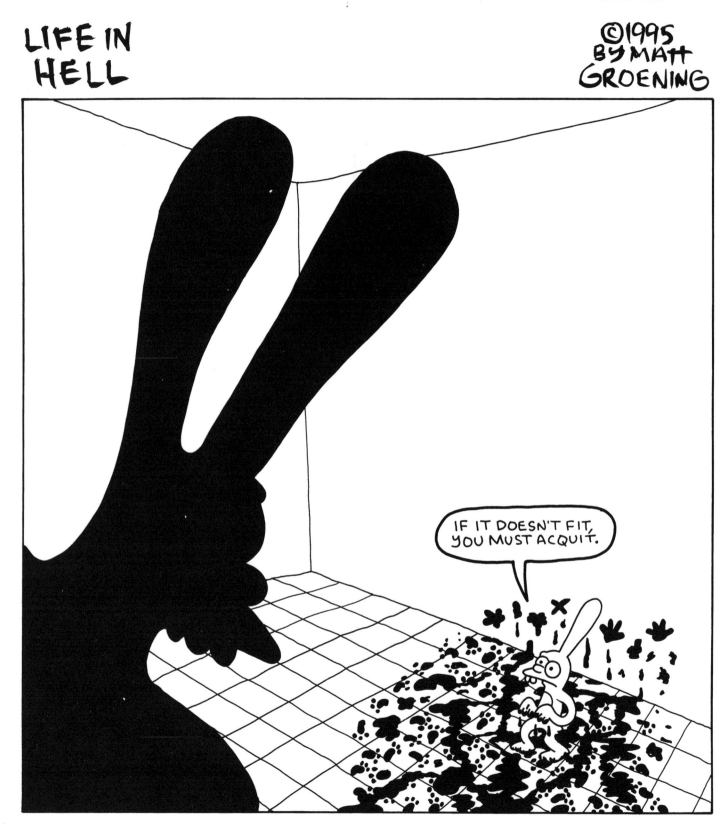

LIFE'S LITTLE BURDENS

AWRIGHT THAT DOES IT. GO TO YOUR ROOM.

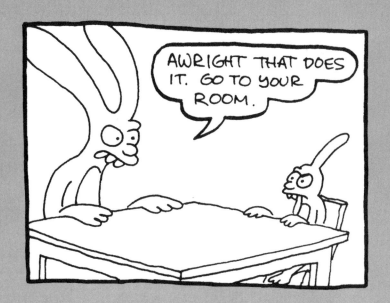

LIFE IN HELL

©1991 BY
MATT
GROENING

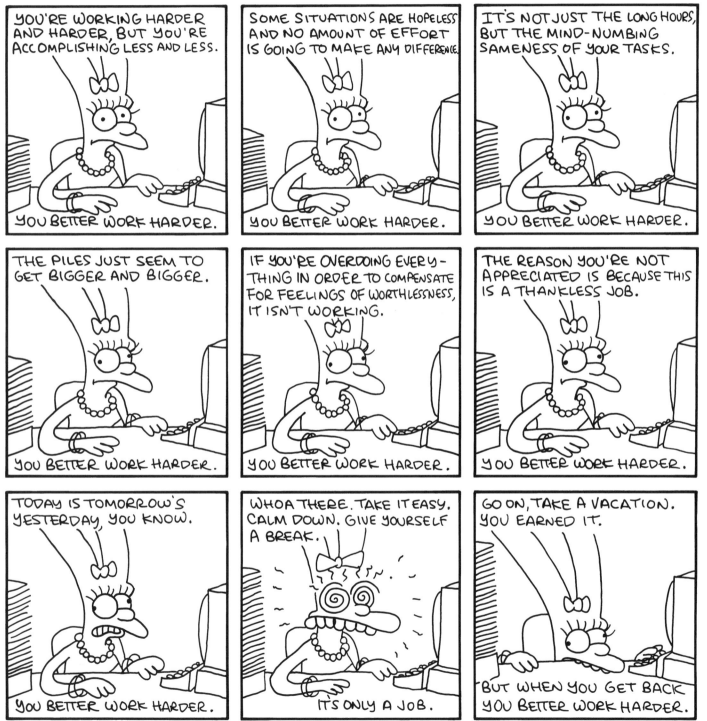

LIFE IN HELL
©1991 BY MATT GROENING
WOULD YOU STILL LOVE ME IF I TESTED POSITIVE?
MAYBE.
WOULD YOU STILL LOVE ME IF I TESTED POSITIVE?
MAYBE.

LIFE IN HELL
©1991 BY MATT GROENING
LOOK HOW MUCH EASIER YOUR LIFE COULD BE IF YOU'D JUST COOPERATE.

LIFE IN HELL
HOW SCREWED UP ARE YOU?
©1982 BY MATT GROENING
YOU EVER FEEL VAGUELY UNEASY, SLIGHTLY DISSATISFIED, OR JUST PLAIN OUT OF SORTS? YOUR PROBLEM IS SIMPLE AND EASILY EXPLAINED: YOU'RE SCREWED UP. BUT HOW SCREWED UP ARE YOU? ARE YOU JUST A BIT SCREWED UP, OR ARE YOU REALLY SCREWED UP? THIS SCIENTIFIC MULTIPLE-CHOICE TEST HAS ALL THE ANSWERS. USE THE HIDDEN PENCIL SUPPLIED WITH THIS PUBLICATION AND BEGIN RIGHT NOW. GO.
MARK THE BOX BELOW THAT MOST CLOSELY APPROXIMATES YOUR CURRENT MOOD. SPEED IS OF THE ESSENCE. CHECK AS MANY BOXES AS YOU FEEL APPLY TO YOU RIGHT NOW. DO NOT RUSH. MARK ONLY ONE BOX.
SCREWY
☐ I AM DISCOURAGED BY DIRECTIONS I DO NOT UNDERSTAND.
☐ WHERE IS MY HIDDEN PENCIL?
☐ NO SPEAK ENGLISH.
☐ I AM A COMPLETE FAILURE.
☐ MY LIFE IS FULL OF HIDDEN PENCILS.
☐ I WANT TO RUN AWAY AND JOIN THE CIRCUS.
☐ IF I COULD ONLY FIND THAT HIDDEN PENCIL, THEN EVERYTHING WOULD BE OKAY.
☐ WHO AM I KIDDING? I AM BAD.
☐ I REFUSE TO BE CHEERED UP.
☐ THINGS ARE GETTING WORSE.
☐ WE'RE ALL DOOMED.
☐ PSYCHOLOGICAL TESTS ARE UNIMPORTANT WHEN THE WORLD IS GOING TO HELL IN A HANDBASKET.
☐ I'VE GOT TO CHEER UP.
☐ RONALD REAGAN IS GOING TO KILL US ALL.
☐ RONALD REAGAN IS GOING TO KILL JUST SOME OF US.
☐ THINGS AREN'T AS FUN AS THEY USED TO BE.
☐ WE CAN WIN WORLD WAR III.
☐ HALP!!!
INTERPRETING YOUR SCORE
1-10 YOU ARE LIVING IN A STATE OF EXTREME ALIENATION. VERY SCREWED UP.
11-20 UH OH. BAD NEWS. HERE COMES TROUBLE. VERY VERY SCREWED UP.
21-30 AVERAGE SCORE. VERY VERY VERY SCREWED UP.
30+ LEAVE THE PLANET IMMEDIATELY.

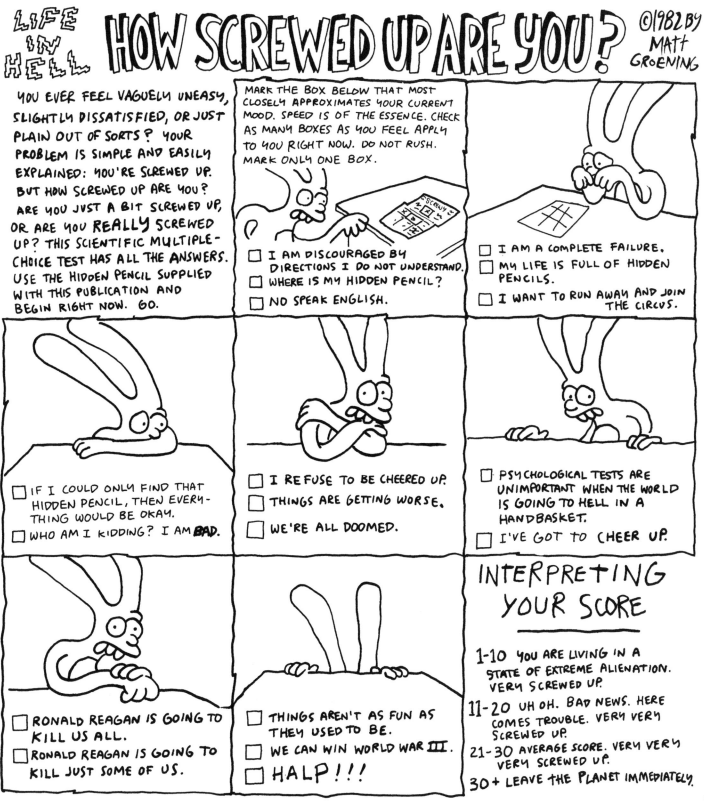

LIFE IN HELL
©1995 BY MATT GROENING
HAPPY BIRTHDAY, ABE!!
DON'T SING.
HOW DOES IT FEEL TO BE FOUR YEARS OLD?
IT FEELS FINE.
WILL, DO YOU HAVE ANY ADVICE FOR ABE NOW THAT HE'S FOUR?
ABE, YOU'RE NOT A BABY ANYMORE. YOU'RE A BOY.
YOU CAN BE GOODER AT VIDEO GAMES. I MEAN BETTER.
YOU DON'T HAVE TO BE IN A CARSEAT ANYMORE.
YOU'RE BIGGER THAN LAST TIME.
YOU CAN REACH UP MORE HIGHER PLACES.
YOU'LL BE BIGGER THAN GODZILLA.
JUST JOKIN'.
YOU CAN STAY UP LATER.
YOUR HAIR IS GOING TO GET DARKER LIKE MINE.
BUT YOU STILL CAN'T DRIVE A CAR.
YOU CAN'T HIDE IN AS MANY SMALL PLACES.
AND YOU'RE STILL MY LITTLE BROTHER. I'LL ALWAYS BE OLDER THAN YOU.
ALWAYS.
ABE, ARE YOU GOING TO USE YOUR NEW POWERS FOR GOOD OR FOR EVIL?
SAY EVIL, ABE.
GOOD.

© 1990 BY MATT GROENING

HOW TO OVERCOME STRESS AT WORK

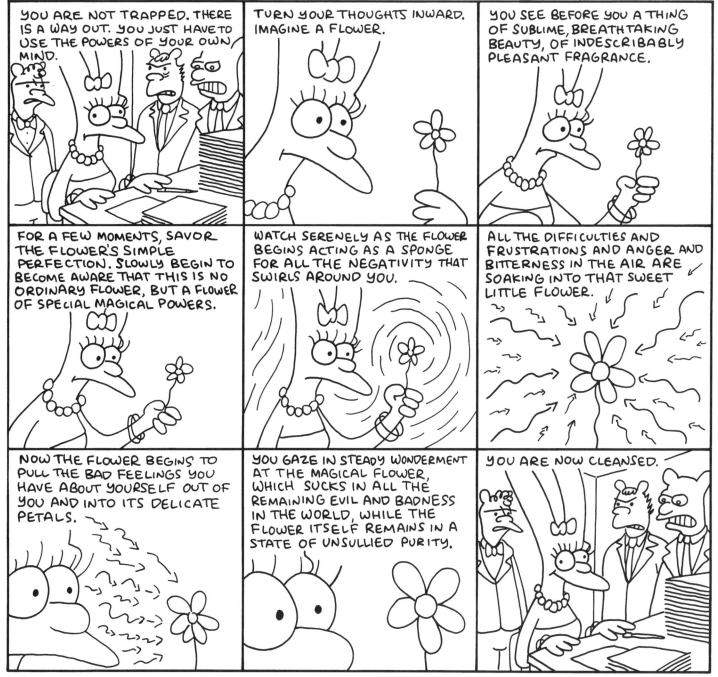

THE LIGHTER SIDE OF HELL

AWRIGHT THAT DOES IT. GO TO YOUR ROOM.
SLAM
NO TRESPASSING
MR. T
"DAD"
STOP
SHARK MOUNTAIN
FASCIST.

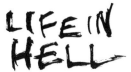

LIFE IN HELL

© 1995 BY MATT GROENING

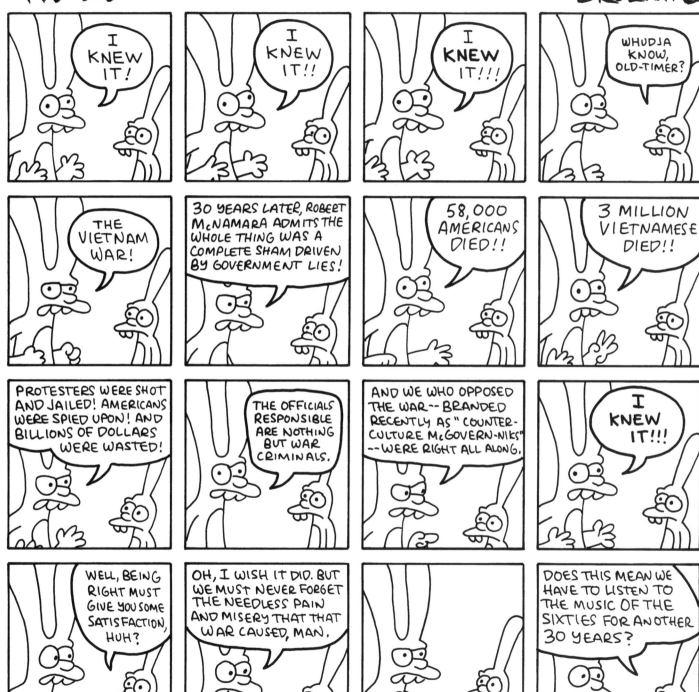

39

LIFE IN HELL
©1996 BY MATT GROENING
I'M SO TIRED.
I'M MORE TIRED THAN YOU.
I'M CHRONICALLY TIRED.
I'M GENETICALLY TIRED.
I'VE BEEN TIRED FOR WEEKS.
I'VE BEEN TIRED FOR MONTHS.
I'VE BEEN TIRED FOR YEARS.
I'VE BEEN TIRED MY WHOLE LIFE.
I'VE BEEN REALLY TIRED DURING EACH OF MY PAST LIVES.
I'M TIRED BECAUSE OF MY FIGHT AGAINST TYRANNY AND INJUSTICE ACROSS THE LAND.
I'M TIRED BECAUSE I CARRY THE WORLD'S SORROWS ON MY SHOULDERS.
I'M TIRED BECAUSE I DIDN'T GET MUCH SLEEP LAST NIGHT.
I'M TIRED BECAUSE I FEEL A COSMIC CONNECTION TO THE CONCEPT OF ENTROPY.
I'M TIRED BECAUSE, ON A DEEPLY PERSONAL LEVEL, I CAN RELATE TO THE IMPENDING HEAT DEATH OF THE UNIVERSE.
FINE. NEITHER OF US WILL CHANGE THE CAT BOX.

LIFE IN HELL
©1995 BY MATT GROENING
WHY DO THE REPUBLICANS WANT TO WEAKEN OUR ENVIRONMENTAL LAWS?
THE AIR STINKS.
THE WATER IS POLLUTED.
THE FISH ARE DYING.
THE LANDSCAPE IS MUTILATED.
GARBAGE IS PILING UP.
TOXIC WASTE GETS DUMPED, LEAKED, AND SPILLED.
HOW MUCH UGLIER AND SMELLIER AND DEADLIER DOES THE WORLD HAVE TO GET BEFORE WE HAVE HAD ENOUGH?
YOU OUGHTA MOVE TO A BETTER NEIGHBORHOOD.

LIFE IN HELL
©1994 BY MATT GROENING
THAT ICE CREAM IS GONNA KILL YOU.
THAT COFFEE IS GONNA KILL YOU.
THAT BUTTER IS GONNA KILL YOU.
THAT MEAT IS GONNA KILL YOU.
THAT DIET DRINK IS GONNA KILL YOU.
THAT SALT IS GONNA KILL YOU.
THAT SUN IS GONNA KILL YOU.
THAT EGG IS GONNA KILL YOU.
R.I.P.
I TOLD YA

LIFE IN HELL
©1994 BY MATT GROENING
ALL RIGHT, WHICH ONE OF YOU DIDN'T TAKE YOUR PROZAC?

LIFE WITH THE FLU

© 1993 BY MATT GROENING

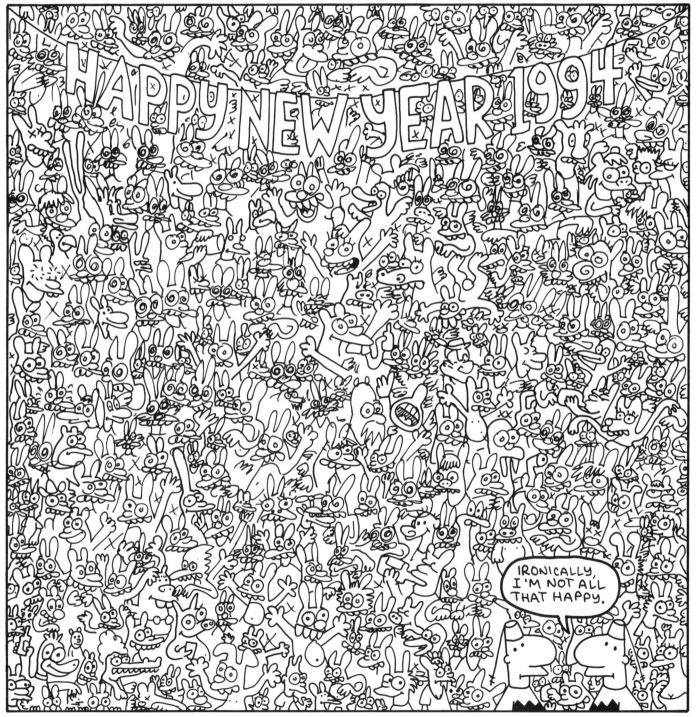

LIFE IN HELL

©1990 BY MATT GROENING

HOW TO HANDLE OVERWHELMING STRESS

KEEP THINGS IN PERSPECTIVE. LIFE CAN SEEM MUCH WORSE WHEN YOU ARE IMMERSED IN YOUR OWN PETTY PROBLEMS.
HEY BINKLES!! THEY'RE TOWIN' YOUR CAR!
BINKY! IN THE BOSS'S OFFICE-- ON THE DOUBLE.
GUESS WHAT! I'M PREGNANT!!
WHERZA 50 BUCKS YOU OWE ME?
TRY TO MODIFY YOUR STRESSFUL SITUATION. YOU PROBABLY WON'T BE ABLE TO COMPLETELY CHANGE THINGS, BUT EVEN A SMALL CHANGE MAY CHEER YOU UP A BIT.
SORRY-- I'M ALLERGIC TO FLOWERS.
MEET YOUR STRESS HEAD-ON. TALK ABOUT THE PROBLEM WITH THOSE AROUND YOU.
I'M FLIPPING OUT, GUYS.
STAY IN YOUR OWN CUBICLE, PLEASE.
TAKE SOME TIME OFF DURING THE WORK DAY.
DO SOME STRETCHES. YOU'LL BE SURPRISED WHAT A LITTLE BODY MOVEMENT CAN HAVE ON YOUR DISPOSITION.
OOOCH.
OWCH.
OOOOOF.
GET ORGANIZED. NOTHING ADDS TO STRESS LIKE A SLOPPY WORKING AREA.
FACE REALITY. YOU MAY VERY WELL BE TRAPPED IN A HORRIBLE, NO-WIN PREDICAMENT. SOMETIMES ACKNOWLEDGING THIS MAY HELP YOU SLIGHTLY.
I'M TRAPPED. I'M DOOMED. IT'S ALL OVER. THERE'S NO HOPE. WOE IS ME. I'M A GONER. MY LIFE IS FINISHED. ALL FUN IS CURTAILED. THAT'S ALL, FOLKS. HELP ME.
RETREATING INTO FANTASY OFTEN HELPS IN AN INTOLERABLE SITUATION.
YOU'RE FIRED!
IF ALL ELSE FAILS, ACHIEVE INNER PEACE.
DAMN. I FORGOT MY MANTRA.

LIFE IN HELL

©1996 BY MATT GROENING

NEW YORK CAB RIDE
A TRUE STORY
I'D LIKE TO GO TO THE IMAX THEATRE ON BROADWAY AT 68th STREET, PLEASE.
COODJU SIGN MY BART SIMPSON DOLL, MR. GROANY? I BIN WAITIN' OUTSIDE YER HOTEL FER HOURS!
HERE YOU GO....
HEY! COME BACK WITH MY PEN!
DO YOU LIKE INDIAN MUSIC, MY FRIEND?
I LOVE INDIAN MUSIC.
THEN LISTEN TO THIS TAPE OF A MOST BEAUTIFUL SONG. I WILL DO THE TRANSLATING FOR YOU.
YOU ARE GOING TO DIE! YOU ARE GOING TO DIE! YOU LIVE IN THE DEN OF DELUSION, AND YOU ARE GOING TO DIE!
YOU MAY BE YOUNG AND ADDICTED TO PLEASURES, YOU MAY BE A SERVANT OR OWN A HUNDRED ELEPHANTS, IT DOES NOT MATTER -- YOU ARE GOING TO DIE!
WHY DO YOU SUCCUMB TO DESIRE? WHY ARE YOU SO DELUDED? WHY DO YOU RUN ABOUT LIKE A FRIGHTENED GHOST? YOU ARE GOING TO DIE!
WHY DO YOU WEEP AND MOAN, MY FRIEND? BECAUSE OF OLD AGE FOR YOU! BECAUSE YOU WILL BE DEFORMED! BECAUSE YOU WILL LOSE YOUR YOUTH! AND YOUR TEETH! AND YOUR MIND! YOU ARE GOING TO DIE!
YOU CAN ENJOY YOUR PRETTY DANCING DAMSELS AND YOUR SWEET CLARIFIED BUTTER, BUT YOU ARE ENCHAINED WITH THE ATTACHMENT OF WORLDLY THINGS, AND YOU ARE GOING TO DIE!
YOU ARE GOING TO DIE! YOU ARE GOING TO DIE! YOU ARE GOING TO DIE!
HERE YOU GO, MY FRIEND: "DIE HARD 3."
I'M NOT GOING TO "DIE HARD 3."
OH YES YOU ARE!

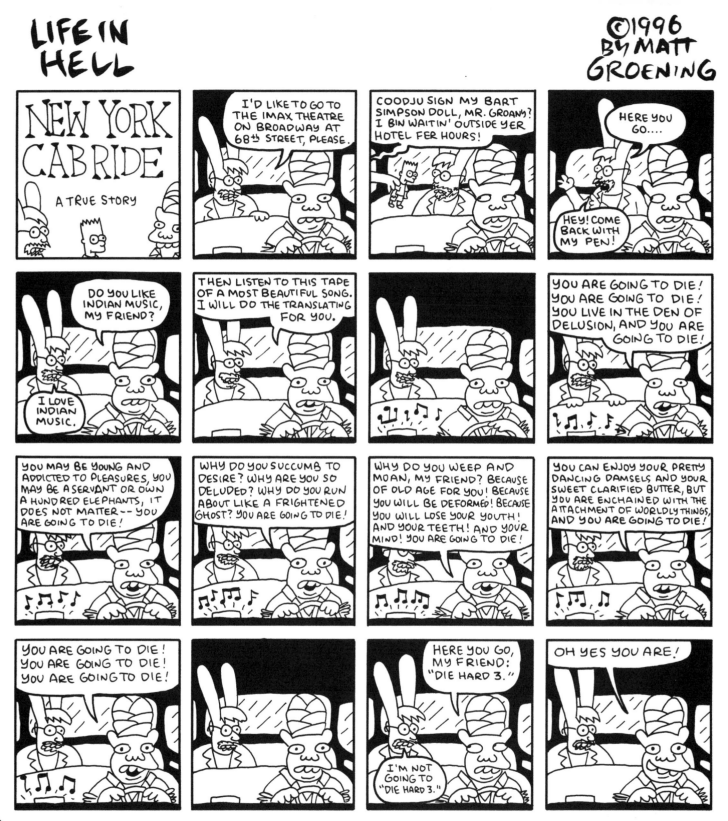

FAMILY LIFE

MONKEYS WILL NEVER GET IN THE HOUSE.
ZZK ZZK ZZK

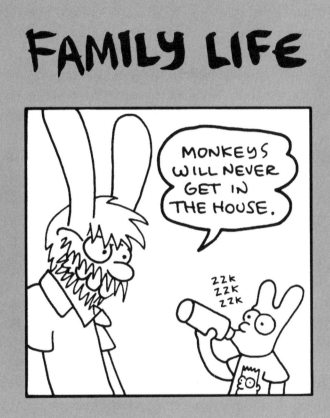

LIFE IN HELL

YUCKY BABY!
AW, DON'T SAY YUCKY BABY. THIS IS A CUTE BABY.
YUCKY BABY! YUCKY BABY!
DADDY! COME HERE!
I WILL. IN A SECOND.
YUCKY BABY!
YUCKY BABY! YUCKY BABY!
SWEET BABY, NOT YUCKY BABY.
YUCKY BABY!
WOW!
YARRGH!
YUCKY DADDY

LIFE IN HELL

'FRAID MONKEYS.
I KNOW YOU'RE AFRAID OF MONKEYS RIGHT NOW.
ZZK ZZK ZZK
BUT WHEN YOU'RE OLDER, YOU WON'T BE AFRAID OF MONKEYS.
ZZK ZZK ZZK
MONKEYS WILL NEVER GET IN THE HOUSE.
ZZK ZZK ZZK
THEY LIVE FAR, FAR AWAY.
ZZK ZZK ZZK
THEY LIVE IN TREES IN THE JUNGLE.
ZZK ZZK ZZK
MOMMY AND DADDY WILL ALWAYS PROTECT YOU. OK?
ZZK ZZK ZZK
OK?
ZZK ZZK ZZK
'FRAID BUNNIES.

LIFE IN HELL
©1991 BY MATT GROENING
IT'S CALLED "RESPECT YOUR ELDERS."

LIFE IN HELL
©1991 BY MATT GROENING
THINGS DAD SAID
THINGS I SAY
THINGS DAD SAID
THINGS I SAY
HEY! DON'T MESS WITH MY TOOLS.
HEY! DON'T MESS WITH MY TOYS.
PLAY YOUR DRUMS MORE QUIETLY!
TURN YOUR DRUM MACHINE OFF WHEN YOU'RE DONE WITH IT!
HAVEN'T YOU WATCHED ENOUGH CARTOONS FOR ONE DAY?
C'MERE QUICK! CARTOONS ARE ON!
WHEN I WAS A BOY THIS USED TO BE BEAUTIFUL COUNTRYSIDE.
NONE OF THESE UGLY BUILDINGS WERE HERE.
WHEN I WAS A BOY THIS USED TO BE A BUNCH OF NEAT BUILDINGS.
NONE OF THESE UGLY MINIMALLS WERE HERE.
WHERE'S MOMMY? GO FIND MOMMY.
WHERE'S MOMMY? GO FIND MOMMY.
WHY? BECAUSE I SAID SO, THAT'S WHY.
WHY? BECAUSE, UM... PLEASE... I'M BEGGING YOU.
NO TOY IS WORTH $49.95.
NO TOY IS WORTH $279.95.
NO, WE'RE NOT THERE YET.
NO, WE'RE NOT THERE YET.

©1985 BY MATT GROENING

SHOULD YOU **REALLY** HAVE A BABY?

A WEE TEST

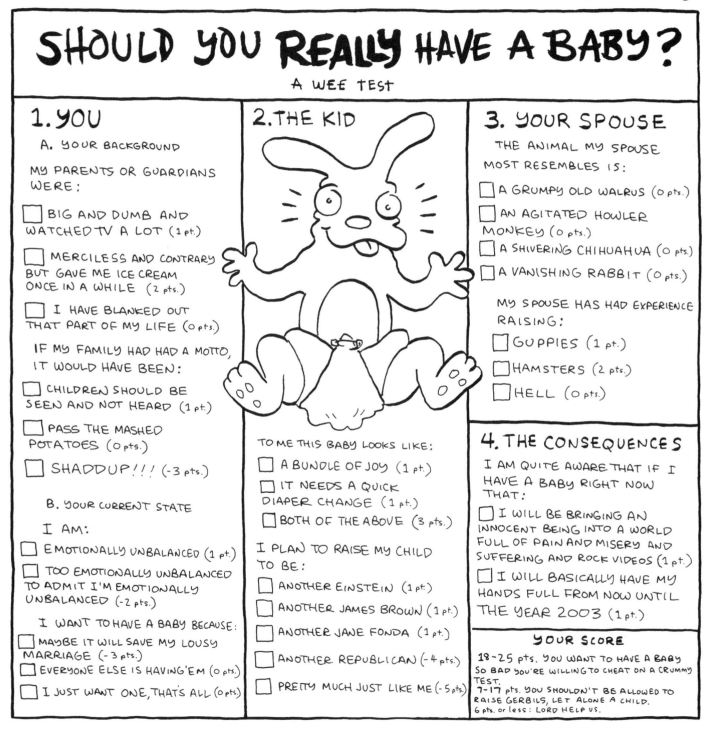

1. YOU

A. YOUR BACKGROUND

MY PARENTS OR GUARDIANS WERE:

- ☐ BIG AND DUMB AND WATCHED TV A LOT (1 pt.)
- ☐ MERCILESS AND CONTRARY BUT GAVE ME ICE CREAM ONCE IN A WHILE (2 pts.)
- ☐ I HAVE BLANKED OUT THAT PART OF MY LIFE (0 pts.)

IF MY FAMILY HAD HAD A MOTTO, IT WOULD HAVE BEEN:

- ☐ CHILDREN SHOULD BE SEEN AND NOT HEARD (1 pt.)
- ☐ PASS THE MASHED POTATOES (0 pts.)
- ☐ SHADDUP!!! (-3 pts.)

B. YOUR CURRENT STATE

I AM:

- ☐ EMOTIONALLY UNBALANCED (1 pt.)
- ☐ TOO EMOTIONALLY UNBALANCED TO ADMIT I'M EMOTIONALLY UNBALANCED (-2 pts.)

I WANT TO HAVE A BABY BECAUSE:

- ☐ MAYBE IT WILL SAVE MY LOUSY MARRIAGE (-3 pts.)
- ☐ EVERYONE ELSE IS HAVING'EM (0 pts.)
- ☐ I JUST WANT ONE, THAT'S ALL (0 pts.)

2. THE KID

TO ME THIS BABY LOOKS LIKE:

- ☐ A BUNDLE OF JOY (1 pt.)
- ☐ IT NEEDS A QUICK DIAPER CHANGE (1 pt.)
- ☐ BOTH OF THE ABOVE (3 pts.)

I PLAN TO RAISE MY CHILD TO BE:

- ☐ ANOTHER EINSTEIN (1 pt.)
- ☐ ANOTHER JAMES BROWN (1 pt.)
- ☐ ANOTHER JANE FONDA (1 pt.)
- ☐ ANOTHER REPUBLICAN (-4 pts.)
- ☐ PRETTY MUCH JUST LIKE ME (-5 pts.)

3. YOUR SPOUSE

THE ANIMAL MY SPOUSE MOST RESEMBLES IS:

- ☐ A GRUMPY OLD WALRUS (0 pts.)
- ☐ AN AGITATED HOWLER MONKEY (0 pts.)
- ☐ A SHIVERING CHIHUAHUA (0 pts.)
- ☐ A VANISHING RABBIT (0 pts.)

MY SPOUSE HAS HAD EXPERIENCE RAISING:

- ☐ GUPPIES (1 pt.)
- ☐ HAMSTERS (2 pts.)
- ☐ HELL (0 pts.)

4. THE CONSEQUENCES

I AM QUITE AWARE THAT IF I HAVE A BABY RIGHT NOW THAT:

- ☐ I WILL BE BRINGING AN INNOCENT BEING INTO A WORLD FULL OF PAIN AND MISERY AND SUFFERING AND ROCK VIDEOS (1 pt.)
- ☐ I WILL BASICALLY HAVE MY HANDS FULL FROM NOW UNTIL THE YEAR 2003 (1 pt.)

YOUR SCORE

18-25 pts. YOU WANT TO HAVE A BABY SO BAD YOU'RE WILLING TO CHEAT ON A CRUMMY TEST.

7-17 pts. YOU SHOULDN'T BE ALLOWED TO RAISE GERBILS, LET ALONE A CHILD.

6 pts. or less: LORD HELP US.

LIFE IN HELL

WILL EXPLAINS CARTOONS
FEATURING THE SONG STYLINGS OF ABE
MY WHOLE LIFE I HAVE WATCHED 50 MILLION CARTOONS SO I CAN TELL YOU ALL ABOUT IT!
THERE ARE FOUR TYPES OF CARTOONS: LOONEY TUNES, TOM & JERRY, DISNEY, AND CLASSICS.
CLASSICS ARE CARTOONS THAT ARE MOSTLY BLACK & WHITE. THEY HAVE LOTS OF ANIMALS THAT BOUNCE UP AND DOWN AT THE SAME TIME.
BOSCO, FLIP THE FROG, AND FELIX THE CAT ARE SOME OF MY FAVORITES. WELL, BOSCO IS KIND OF BAD. FLIP THE FROG PLAYS PIANO AND MAKES FUNNY TUNES WITH HIS MOUTH. FELIX JUST SHOWS A PICTURE OF FELIX. SILENT FELIX IS KIND OF GOOD TO MY DAD BUT NOT TO ME.
TOM & JERRY IS ABOUT A CAT THAT IS ALWAYS TRYING TO KILL A MOUSE. BUT WHAT THE CAT DOESN'T KNOW IS THAT THE MOUSE IS A MASTERMIND GENIUS.
DISNEY HAS MICKEY MOUSE. HE SEEMS LIKE A GOOD MAIN CHARACTER, BUT HE REALLY ISN'T. HE JUST GOES "HA-HA" ALL THE TIME.
DONALD DUCK IS JUST COMPLAINING ALL THE TIME. PLUTO JUST GETS MAD ALL THE TIME. AND GOOFY DOESN'T KNOW WHAT'S GOING ON.
IN LOONEY TUNES, THE ACTORS ARE THE HUNTERS AND THE NONHUNTERS. LET'S SAY THE HUNTER IS ELMER FUDD AND THE NONHUNTER IS BUGS BUNNY. MANY PEOPLE DON'T LIKE BUGS BUNNY: ELMER, DAFFY DUCK, COYOTE, AND YOSEMITE SAM.
DAFFY DUCK IS A REAL CRAZY DUCK. ROAD RUNNER IS KIND OF BAD. IT WOULD BE MORE FUNNER IF COYOTE GOT THE ROADRUNNER SOMETIMES.
LOTS OF CARTOON CHARACTERS HAVE MAIN WORDS. FRED FLINTSTONE'S MAIN WORD IS "YABBADABBADOO." BUGS BUNNY'S MAIN WORD IS "WHAT'S UP DOC?" HOMER SIMPSON'S MAIN WORD IS "D'OH."
THERE'S ALSO BETTY BOOP. SHE'S A VERY STRANGE CHARACTER. THE SIZE OF HER HEAD IS KIND OF WEIRD.
I LOVE PIE-PIE!
POPEYE.
OH YEAH. POPEYE.
BUT OUR MOM DOESN'T LIKE THE RUDE SONG.
♪ I'M POPEYE THE SAILOR MAN
I LIVE IN A GARBAGE CAN
I TURNED ON THE HEATER ♫
AND BURNED OFF MY WIENER
I'M POPEYE THE SAILOR MAN
♪ POOP POOP!
WE LIKE CARTOONS BECAUSE THEY ARE FUNNY.
AND BECAUSE WE GET TO WATCH THREE OF THEM BEFORE BEDTIME!

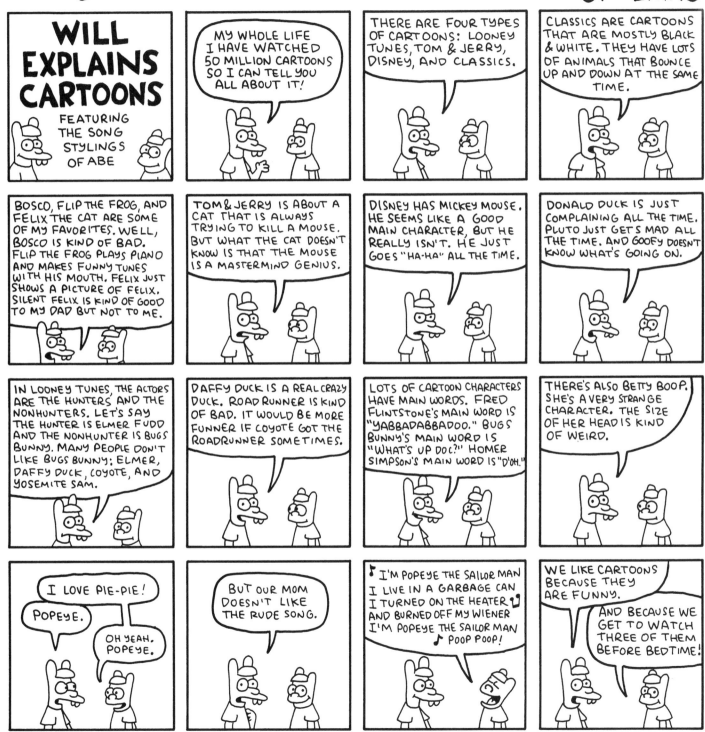

LIFE IN HELL

©1986 BY MATT GROENING

WHAT TO NAME THE BABY

CAN'T DECIDE ON A NAME? THEN WHY NOT GIVE IT AN AFFECTIONATE PET-NAME?

JUNIOR	BUNNY
CUTEMS	PEE-WEE
SQUIRT	SPROUT
KIDKINS	KIDLET
JOY BOY	SNOOKUMS
SQUIDLY	DROOLY

A REAL NAME SHOULD BE CHOSEN BY THE TIME THE YOUNGSTER REACHES 16 YEARS OF AGE OR EMOTIONAL DAMAGE MAY RESULT.

WHY NOT LET YOUR CHILD KNOW WHAT IS EXPECTED OF HIM OR HER IN LATER LIFE WITH THE NAME OF SOMEONE IMPORTANT?

BO	WHOOPI
BING	HEF
DIZZY	YO-YO
FATS	ZBIGNIEW
FIDEL	RINGO
OZZIE	MOTHRA
OZZY	JESUS
ZSA ZSA	ZEPPO

HOW ABOUT A NAME FROM THE WORLD OF CARTOONS OR SPORTS?

	YOGI
ZONKER	SNOOPY
KAREEM	DAGWOOD
GOOSE	BAMBI
BOOG	BUBBA
SNUFFY	PRUNEFACE

BELOVED BRAND NAMES MAKE FOR DISTINCTIVE AND UNUSUAL MONIKERS!

PEPSI	MCNUGGET
BEATRICE	FRIGIDAIRE
	AQUAFRESH
	PURINA

HOW ABOUT A NAME FROM THE BIBLE?

ZADOK	
FESTUS	
DUMAH	ZUPH
HOTHAN	AGAG
PENNINAH	ZAZA
SHEBA	GOG
SHEBER	BEELZEBUB
SHEBAM	MADMANNAH
ONAN	BONGO
ABITUB	SHITRAH
PISPAH	ZEEB

DO YOU DESIRE A TOUGH, MASCULINE SON? THEN TRY: GRUMPY MAD MAX

BUSTER	BUTCH	ELVIS
AKBAR	ROCKY	BINKY

WANT TO RAISE A SWEET, FEMININE GAL? HOW ABOUT:

COOKIE
FAWN
CANDY   KITTEN   OBEDIENTA
HONEY   FLUFFY   PRINCESS

THE FOLLOWING NAMES ARE NO LONGER RECOMMENDED:

ADOLPH	
REMUS	
SIRHAN	HORTENSE
MILHOUS	POINDEXTER
LOLITA	EGBERT
FANNY	GOMER
	ORAL

54

PARLOR TRICKS

LIFE IN HELL
©1996 BY MATT GROENING
WELCOME YOUNG REPUBLICANS
WHOOPS. WRONG PARTY.

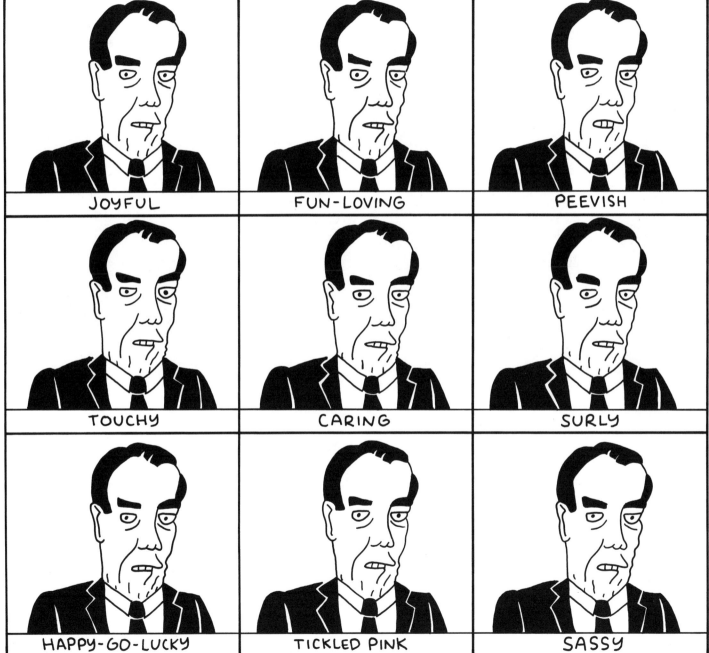

LIFE IN HELL

©1996 BY MATT GROENING

THE MANY MOODS OF BOB DOLE

JOYFUL	FUN-LOVING	PEEVISH
TOUCHY	CARING	SURLY
HAPPY-GO-LUCKY	TICKLED PINK	SASSY

LIFE IN HELL
©1996 BY MATT GROENING
WISDOM OF THE AGES
1960s
WE HAD TO DESTROY THE VILLAGE IN ORDER TO SAVE IT.
1970s
WATERGATE IS PROOF THAT THE SYSTEM WORKS.
1980s
HELPING THE RICH IS HELPING THE POOR.
1990s
BY BEING THE SAME AS REPUBLICANS WE CAN DEFEAT THE REPUBLICANS.

LIFE IN HELL
©1995 BY MATT GROENING
STREET SMARTS FOR REPUBLICANS
BE CAREFUL OUT THERE.
IT MAY SEEM LIKE A REPUBLICAN WORLD, BUT THERE ARE STILL MANY PEOPLE WHO DON'T REALIZE THEY AREN'T NORMAL.
AVOID AREAS OF TOWN WHERE THE BURDEN OF WELFARE HAS BEEN LIFTED. THE LOCALS JUST AREN'T GRATEFUL YET.
DON'T BOTHER EXPLAINING HOW GETTING RID OF AFFIRMATIVE ACTION WILL END RACISM AND DISCRIMINATION IN AMERICA ONCE AND FOR ALL.
DO NOT SAY THIS:
DON'T WHITE MALES DESERVE A FAIR SHAKE FOR ONCE??
THEY JUST WON'T UNDERSTAND.
BEWARE OF HOMOSEXUALS AND THEIR RADICAL GAY AGENDA, DARK-SKINNED ILLEGAL IMMIGRANTS WHO DON'T EVEN SPEAK ENGLISH, AND COUNTERCULTURE McGOVERNIKS HAVING SEX AND ABORTIONS JUST FOR THE FUN OF IT.
IF YOU SEE ANY SMALL STREET URCHINS WHO LOOK LIKE THEY DON'T HAVE WEAPONS, YOU MIGHT CONSIDER CHEERING THEM UP WITH THE GOOD NEWS OF REPUBLICAN REFORMS.
HEY, POOR KIDS! THERE'LL BE NO MORE FREE SCHOOL LUNCHES, BUT SOON YOU'LL BE ABLE TO PRAY IN SCHOOL FOR ANYTHING YOU WANT-- EVEN FOOD!!
AND ALWAYS REMEMBER TO BE A CARING REPUBLICAN.
STEP OVER THE HOMELESS, NOT ON THEM.

LIFE IN HELL
©1994 BY MATT GROENING
I HOPE YOU REALIZE THAT THE MORE YOU CALL REPUBLICANS HATEFUL AND UNCARING, THE LONGER YOU'LL HAVE TO STAY IN THE ORPHANAGE.

LIFE IN HELL
©1994 BY MATT GROENING
WHAT THE HELL IS WRONG WITH THIS COUNTRY?
ARE WE REALLY AS GREEDY, ARROGANT, AND BIGOTED AS THE REPUBLICANS ON TV?
DO WE REALLY HAVE NO COMPASSION FOR MINORITIES, THE POOR, OR ANYONE WHO'S DIFFERENT?
DO WE REALLY HATE FUNDING THE ARTS? DO WE REALLY WANT TO TAKE AWAY EQUAL RIGHTS FOR GAYS? DO WE REALLY WANT TO PUNISH THE CHILDREN OF ILLEGAL IMMIGRANTS BY NOT ALLOWING THEM MEDICAL TREATMENT?
DO WE REALLY NEED TO BUILD MORE PRISONS INSTEAD OF SCHOOLS?
DO WE REALLY NEED LESS GUN CONTROL? DO WE REALLY NEED MORE CENSORSHIP? DO WE REALLY NEED THE RIDICULOUSLY EXPENSIVE, UNWORKABLE "3 STRIKES AND YOU'RE OUT" LAWS?
DO WE REALLY WANT TO CONTINUE THE SLOW BUT STEADY SLIDE TOWARDS FASCISM?
HAS ALL THE HATEFUL REPUBLICAN RHETORIC FINALLY CURDLED EVERYONE'S MINDS?
STRIKE ONE.

LIFE IN HELL
©1994 BY MATT GROENING
THE IRAN-CONTRA REPORT IS FINALLY OUT
THAT'S WHY I'M SHOUTING AND DANCING ABOUT!
OLIVER NORTH WAS SOME TESTIFIER
TURNS OUT NORTH WAS A SLEAZEBAG LIAR!
BUT THE SHAMEFUL COVER-UP WENT MUCH, MUCH HIGHER
POINDEXTER WAS ALSO A SLEAZEBAG LIAR!
WEINBERGER, McFARLANE: BOTH FALSIFIERS! PLUS LITTLE ED MEESE: ALL SLEAZEBAG LIARS!
AND WILLIAM J. CASEY, THE HEAD CLASSIFIER
MAY HE REST IN PEACE (HE'S A SLEAZEBAG LIAR!)
AND THEN THERE'S GEORGE BUSH, THE UTTER DENIER
GUESS WHAT, FOLKS? A BIG SLEAZEBAG LIAR!
WHICH BRINGS US RIGHT UP TO THE GREAT SIMPLIFIER
RONALD REAGAN HIMSELF WAS A SLEAZEBAG LIAR!
SO WE ALL KNOW THEY'RE GUILTY, IT'S QUITE DEFINITE--
TOO BAD THEY ALL GOT AWAY WITH IT!

LIFE IN HELL

©1992 BY MATT GROENING

NOW BE HONEST. AREN'T YOU GOING TO MISS THOSE REPUBLICAN SLEAZEBALLS JUST A LITTLE BIT?
NOT REALLY.

LIFE IN HELL
©1992 BY MATT GROENING
HIC
HIC
HIC HIC
HIC
HIC
HIC
HIC
HIC
HIC
HIC HIC HIC
HIC
HIC HIC
FAMILY VALUES.
THANK YOU.

LOVE IS STILL HELL

HEY! IT'S GOT A PULL-STRING.

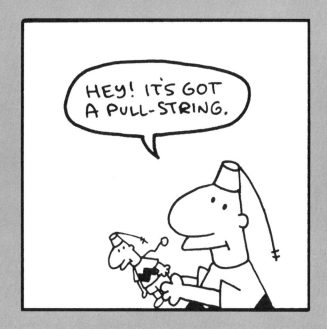

LIFE IN HELL
©1996 BY MATT GROENING
I LOVE YOU.
I LOVE YOU MORE.
I LOVE YOU A BUCKETFUL OF LOVE.
I LOVE YOU A BARRELFUL OF LOVE.
I LOVE YOU A DUMPTRUCK FULL OF LOVE.
I LOVE YOU A SEWAGE TREATMENT PLANT FULL OF LOVE.
I LOVE YOU A SECRET UNDERGROUND TOXIC WASTE DUMP FULL OF LOVE.
I LOVE YOU THE TOWN OF BEAVERTON, OREGON, FULL OF LOVE.
I LOVE YOU THE THE ENTIRE PLANET EARTH FULL OF LOVE.
I LOVE YOU A WHOLE SUPERNOVA FULL OF LOVE.
WELL, NOW YOU'RE EXAGGERATING.
OH GOD, IT'S TRUE. THE TRUTH IS I ONLY LOVE YOU A FEW TINY FOOD PELLETS FULL OF LOVE.
HEY, ME TOO.
SAD, ISN'T IT?
AT LEAST OUR LOVE IS EQUAL.
HOW MANY PELLETS FULL OF LOVE?
MAYBE YOU SHOULDN'T ASK.

LIFE IN HELL
©1991 BY MATT GROENING
DEFINE "LOVE."
LOVE IS HAPPINESS.
VERY GOOD.

LIFE IN HELL

©1996 BY MATT GROENING

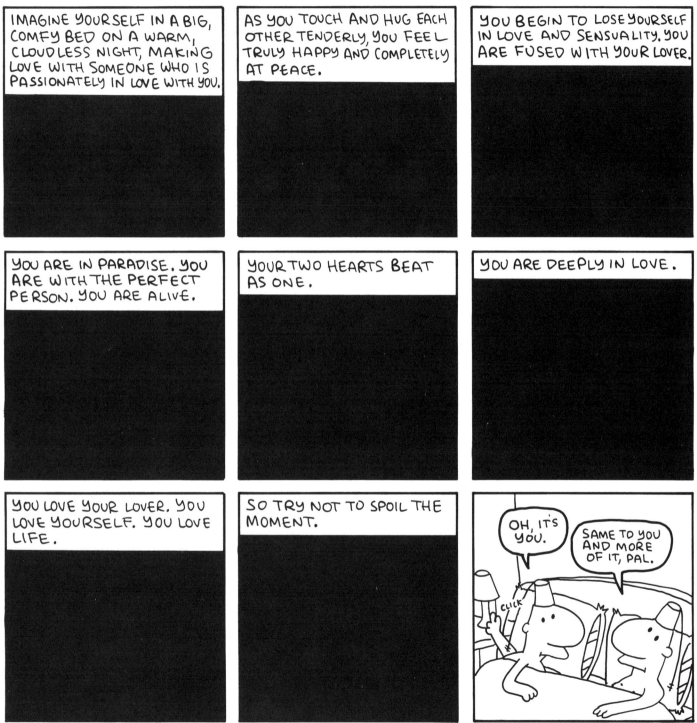

LIFE IN HELL
©1996 BY MATT GROENING
LADIES AND GENTLEMEN, BOYS AND GIRLS: AKBAR COULDN'T BE HERE TODAY. HE'S GOT ONE OF THOSE COLDS THAT'S GOING AROUND.
BUT I'LL TRY TO CARRY ON WITHOUT HIM.
HELLO, YOU HANDSOME DEVIL.
YOU'RE EVER-SO-DESIRABLE.
SMART 'N' SENSITIVE, TOO.
YOU'VE GOT SUCH SOULFUL EYES.
SURELY I'M NOT PERFECT, AM I?
WELL, IF THERE'S ONE TEENY WEENY LITTLE THING I'D CHANGE ABOUT YOU, IT'S YOUR SUDDEN VIOLENT MOOD CHANGES.
YOU SMUG LITTLE JERK.
YOU THINK YOU'RE HOT? WELL, YOU'RE NOT.
QUITE SIMPLY, YOU DISGUST ME.
SIGH.
I'D LIKE TO APOLOGIZE TO THE AUDIENCE. THIS SOLILOQUY BUSINESS JUST ISN'T WORKING. IT'S NOT BELIEVABLE. IT'S NOT REALISTIC. LET'S FACE IT.
I NEED MY AKBAR.
I WONDER HOW HE'S DOING.
YOU WANT MORE THROAT LOZENGES? GET 'EM YOURSELF, PHLEGM-BOY.

LIFE IN HELL
©1995 BY MATT GROENING
HEY! HERE'S AN INTERESTING MAGAZINE ARTICLE: "HOW TO RATE YOUR RELATIONSHIP."
OOH! I LOVE THESE THINGS.
"ON THE FOLLOWING SLIDING SCALE, WHICH OF THESE PHRASES MOST DESCRIBES YOUR RELATIONSHIP?"
"SUPREMELY HAPPY. A PERFECT LOVING COMBINATION OF INDEPENDENCE AND INTIMACY."
"VERY, VERY HAPPY. SOME AREAS NEEDING IMPROVEMENT, BUT ON THE WHOLE INTENSELY PASSIONATE AND LOVING."
"VERY HAPPY. LOTS OF JOY, BUT OCCASIONALLY VAGUE FEELINGS THAT THINGS COULD BE A TAD BETTER."
"SOMEWHAT HAPPY. DAY-TO-DAY FRUSTRATIONS CAN BE VEXING AT TIMES."
"NEITHER HAPPY NOR SAD. A SENSE OF FLATNESS AND BOREDOM VERGING ON NUMBNESS."
"SOMEWHAT UNHAPPY. PETTY POWER STRUGGLES CAN BECOME ANNOYING, FLARING UP INTO LONG, FRUITLESS BICKERING."
"VERY UNHAPPY. CRUEL INSULTS AND BITTER RECRIMINATIONS HURLED WITH ALMOST NIGHTLY REGULARITY."
"VERY, VERY UNHAPPY. PAIN AND MISTRUST ARE DOMINANT FEELINGS. SMALL OBJECTS GET THROWN."
"VERY, VERY, VERY, VERY UNHAPPY. MUTUAL DISRESPECT, MUCH SLAMMING OF DOORS, AND LOTS OF SCREECHING."
"EXTREMELY UNHAPPY. A CHRONIC STATE OF FUMING AND WRATH, WITH HIGH-DECIBEL YELLING. HEFTY SMALL APPLIANCES FLUNG WITH INCREASING ACCURACY."
"SUPREMELY UNHAPPY. UTTER HATRED, COMBINED WITH SKIN-CRAWLING REPUGNANCE. BOTH PARTNERS DEVOTE LIVES TO MAKING THE OTHER MISERABLE."
KEEP GOING.

LIFE IN HELL

©1983 BY MATT GROENING

SEX TOYS FOR THE TRULY ADVENTUROUS

NERVOUS PARROT

TV SET TUNED TO "FLINTSTONES"

C'MON BARNEY

BINKY MASKS

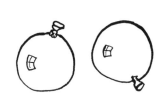

WATER BALLOONS

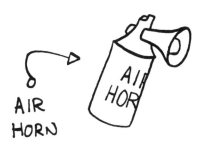

AIR HORN

FUNHOUSE MIRROR

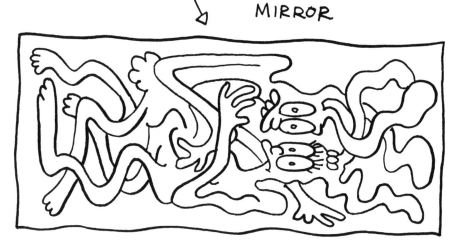

LIFE IN HELL

©1995 BY MATT GROENING

WHAT'S THE WILDEST THING YOU'VE EVER DONE SEXUALLY?
WELL, IT'S KIND OF EMBARRASSING, BUT... I'LL WHISPER IT TO YOU.
YOU SEE, ONE NIGHT I WENT TO THIS EXOTIC MASQUERADE BALL, AND... WHISPER WHISPER WHISPER
OH MY GOSH. GO ON.
AND THEN... WHISPER WHISPER WHISPER
EWWWW.
BUT THEN... WHISPER WHISPER WHISPER
GAH!!!
MEANWHILE... WHISPER WHISPER WHISPER
YEEK!!!
AND THEN... WHISPER WHISPER WHISPER
YUCK!!!
AND THEN, UNBEKNOWNST TO ME... WHISPER WHISPER WHISPER
YOU SICKEN ME.
AND FINALLY... WHISPER WHISPER WHISPER
THAT WAS YOU??

LIFE IN HELL

NOT MANY RELATIONSHIPS COULD WITHSTAND SUCH HONESTY.

LIFE IN HELL
©1996 BY MATT GROENING
DO YOU EVEN LIKE ME, AKBAR? SOMETIMES I WONDER.
A PRESENT?? POUR MOI???
OH MY GOD! IT'S A LITTLE DOLL THAT LOOKS EXACTLY LIKE YOU!
I HAD IT SPECIALLY MADE. I FIND IT HARD TO EXPRESS MY FEELINGS DIRECTLY, SO I THOUGHT A LITTLE DOLL MIGHT HELP.
I LOVE IT, AKBAR! THIS IS THE NICEST, SWEETEST, MOST TOUCHING THING YOU'VE EVER DONE FOR ME.
GOTTA RUN NOW.
HEY! IT'S GOT A PULL-STRING.
MY NAME IS TALKING AKBAR, AND I HAVE EXTREMELY AMBIVALENT FEELINGS ABOUT YOU.

LIFE IN HELL

FOR THE ON-THE-GO POSTFEMINIST SINGLE URBAN CAREER WOMAN OF THE EIGHTIES
Miffed
FALL 1983 $2.95
SPINELESS JELLYFISH AND HUFFING APES
THE TWO MAJOR MALE TYPES
WEIRD HAIRDOS YOU'LL NEVER DARE TRY
THOSE WILD MALE STRIP SHOWS!!!
LIBERATED CULTURAL FREEDOM OR JUST SOMETHING TO GIGGLE ABOUT AT WORK THE NEXT DAY?
HOW TO CONCEAL NUMBED SHOCK WHEN FRIENDS ANNOUNCE MARRIAGE PLANS
"TACKY," "HUNK," "BOZO," AND OTHER ESSENTIAL WORDS TO ADD TO YOUR VOCABULARY
THOSE YUMMY NEW ARTIFICIAL SWEETENERS
THEY DON'T REALLY LIKE CUNNILINGUS, DO THEY?
NUDE PIX OF BIG BEEFY MORONS
THE CONSIDERATE, ATTENTIVE BOYFRIEND
LOVE IDEAL OR IRRITATING WIMP?
BAD NEWS
ABOUT THE BEST-SELLING "HOMEMADE FUDGE BROWNIE DIET"
THAT EXOTIC NEW WAVE SLUT LOOK
GAY MEN
WHY THEY WON'T SLEEP WITH US NO MATTER HOW LONG WE HANG AROUND THEM
HMPH
THE 2 A.M. SCREAMING ARGUMENT
HOW TO MAKE AN AVERAGE RELATIONSHIP DRAMATIC AS HELL
8 BILLION ADS
AND JUST AS MANY SUSPICIOUS EDITORIAL/PICTORIAL PLUGS
SPECIAL BOOK BONUS EXCERPT: "OUR BODS, OUR SELVES"

LIFE IN HELL
©1996 BY MATT GROENING
YOU KNOW WHAT I'D LIKE TO HEAR FROM YOU RIGHT NOW? JUST THREE LITTLE WORDS... THREE ROMANTIC LITTLE WORDS... OH, HOW MY HEART WOULD SING TO HEAR THOSE THREE SWEET LITTLE MAGIC WORDS...
YOU MEAN...
DON'T TOUCH ME?
NO.
WHAT'S THAT ODOR?
NO.
I'M WITH STUPID?
NO.
WHAT A DUMP?
NO.
I LOVE UKELELES?
NO.
GET IT YOURSELF?
NO.
SHUT YER TRAP?
NO.
SO LONG, SUCKER?
NO.
YA BIG DUMMY?
NO.
I LOVE YOU?
NO.
NO?
NO.
I GIVE UP.
AHHH...

LIFE IN HELL
©1995 BY MATT GROENING
HOW CAN I BE SURE YOU REALLY LOVE ME?
WELL, THEY SAY THE EYES ARE WINDOWS TO THE SOUL.
I WANT YOU TO LOOK DEEPLY INTO MY SOUL AND THEN DECIDE HOW I REALLY FEEL ABOUT YOU.
WOW! YOU LOVE ME AS MUCH AS I LOVE YOU.
LET'S NEVER DO THAT AGAIN.

LIFE IN HELL
©1996 BY MATT GROENING
I'VE BEEN STUDYING BODY LANGUAGE LATELY, AND I CAN READ EVERY ONE OF YOUR SECRET THOUGHTS AND HIDDEN FEELINGS.
WOW.
JOY.
DESPAIR.
EXUBERANCE.
REPUGNANCE.
DESIRE.
BITTERNESS.
SERENITY.
ANGER.
PASSION.
FURY.
ENNUI.
THAT WAS INCREDIBLE! YOU CAN READ ME LIKE A BOOK!
ACTUALLY, THOSE WERE MY FEELINGS.

SOUP DU JOUR

MUST YOU SLAP THE BOTTOMS OF YOUR BARE FEET ON THE FLOOR SO LOUDLY?

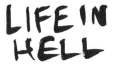

OLD FOLKS' HOME CONVERSATION, 2050 AD

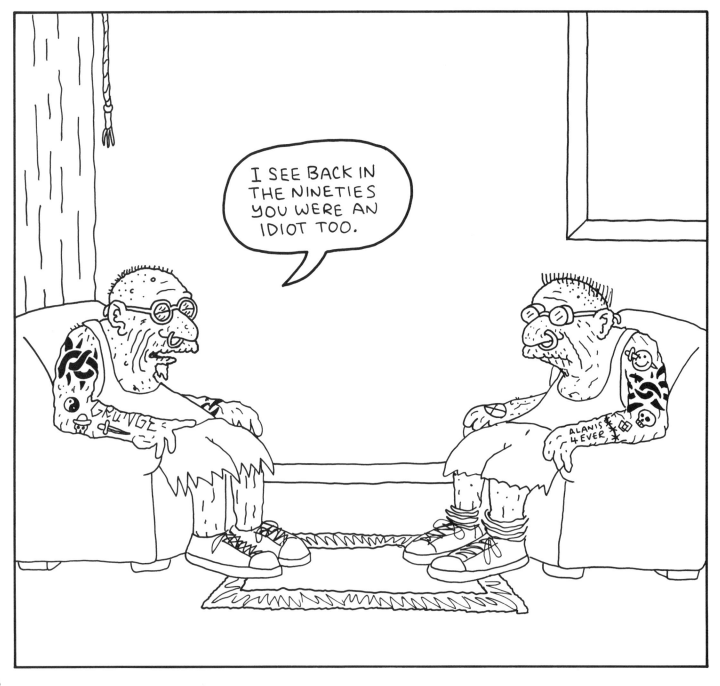

LIFE IN HELL
©1995 BY MATT GROENING
YOU SURE LOOK HAPPY!
OH, I'M MORE THAN HAPPY. I'M FOCUSED. I'M LIVING WITH PURPOSE. I'M ALIVE WITH DEDICATION.
I JUST BOUGHT MYSELF A NEW DAILY PLANNER!
MY WHOLE LIFE IS FINALLY TOTALLY ORGANIZED!
LOOK! IT COMES IN A LUXURIANT LEATHER BINDER.
SEE, HERE'S THE SECTION FOR MY PERSONAL CREDO.
AND THIS PAGE IS FOR MY LIST OF LIFETIME GOALS.
NEXT I HAVE A SPECIAL FOLDER FOR MY FIVE-YEAR PLAN.
IN THESE COLUMNS I PUT MY ORGANIZATIONAL, RECREATIONAL, DIETARY, AND SPIRITUAL PRIORITIES.
THIS SECTION IS FOR READING MY DAILY BUSINESS AFFIRMATIONS.
AND THESE SHEETS ARE FOR MARKING MY PRAYER AND MEDITATION GOALS.
HERE'S MY ACTION FILE, MY URGENT ACTION FILE, AND MY BACK-BURNER FILE.
AND HERE I HAVE MY OWN PERSONALIZED ACHIEVEMENT MANIFESTO THAT I CAN CONSULT ANYTIME I WANT TO!
SOUNDS GREAT, MAN. WHAT'S NEXT ON YOUR "TO DO" LIST?
LET ME SEE....
OOH!! I HAVE TIME FOR A COUPLE GAMES OF TETRIS BEFORE "BAYWATCH" COMES ON.

©1995
BY MATT
GROENING

LIFE IN HELL
©1994 BY MATT GROENING
THANKS TO STEVE VANCE
WON'T YOU HELP US PROFIT FROM THE SUFFERING OF OTHERS?
WE'RE FREEWAY CLOSE! ER... UH...
Akbar & Jeff's Earthquake T-Shirt Hut
FREE SIP OF LIFE-GIVING WATER WITH EVERY PURCHASE!
"BRINGING YOU THE FINEST IN EXPLOITATIVE FUNWEAR SINCE THE 1992 RIOTS"
I USED TO ♥ L.A.
I WATCHED 27 HOURS OF INSIPID LOCAL TV NEWS AND LIVED
I GUESS GOD HATES UGLY ARCHITECTURE
WILL WORK FOR OUT-OF-STATE BUS TICKET
AT LEAST WITH FEWER FREEWAYS WE'LL HAVE FEWER FREEWAY SHOOTINGS
HOW COME NO ONE CARES ABOUT MY SMASHED SNOW DOME COLLECTION?
IF YOU WON'T TELL ME YOUR TEDIOUS EARTHQUAKE STORY, I WON'T TELL YOU MINE
I SURVIVED THE MEDIUM ONE

LIFE IN HELL
©1994 BY MATT GROENING
SHALL WE GO TO THE STORE AND GET SOME EXOTIC OVERPRICED EARLY-DEATH GOURMET ICE CREAM?
BRILLIANT IDEA.
I'M IN THE MOOD FOR SOMETHING SIMPLE YET ELEGANT: RUM 'N' RASPBERRY RHUMBA.
I'M MORE IN THE MOOD FOR TRIPLE-BYPASS FUDGE FREAKOUT.
SORRY, BUT I'VE GOT MY EYE ON HUNKY SPUNKY CANDY-BAR CHUNKY SWIRL-O-RAMA.
BUT I CAN ALREADY TASTE THE DOUBLE-FAT VANILLA BEAN WITH BUTTER BLOBS 'N' CREAM.
I MUST INSIST ON BLUEBERRY PUDDING 'N' JAMOCA GUMBALL SURPRISE.
YOU'RE STARTING TO MAKE ME ANGRY. THE OBVIOUS CHOICE IS SUPER-DUPER SHARDS O' FUDGE 'N' PEANUT BITS.
MY DECISION IS FINAL: BUTTERSCOTCH 'N' TAFFY DOUBLE-SYRUP JUBILEE.
I'LL IGNORE YOUR PETTY INSOLENCE AND MERELY SAY THIS: MOCHA-CHOKE-A WITH EXTRA EGG YOLKA.
LET'S FACE IT. WE'RE HOPELESSLY DEADLOCKED.
I GUESS WE'VE GOT TO LEARN TO COMPROMISE.

LIFE IN HELL
©1991 BY MATT GROENING
I SUPPOSE YOU THINK THIS WILL BUY MY AFFECTION.

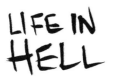

© 1986 BY MATT GROENING

HOW TO UNDERSTAND YOUR BABY'S GIBBERISH

PART ONE

PART TWO LATER

A abba (ă-bə) n. 1. Apple. 2. Swedish pop group (rare).

ahhh (ä) interj. 1. "I am utterly amazed!" 2. "What the hell is going on around here?" 3. "Glory be!"

ammo (am'ō) n. 1. Animal, usu. stuffed, oft. cuddly. 2. Ammunition.

B baby (bā'bē) pron. 1. I, myself, helplessly adrift in a hostile universe.

banky (băng'kē) n. 1. Blanket. 2. Any filthy rag to which an emotional attachment has been made.

baw (bô) n. 1. Bottle. 2. Breast, usu. of mother. 3. Any liquid refreshment.

beh (bĕ) n. 1. Bed. 2. Bird. 3. Boy. 4. Begonia (rare).

boo-boo (boo'boo') n. 1. Any misfortune. 2. "A dreadful error has been made, perhaps due to my own incompetence, but I know you will forgive me because I am so goshdarned cute."

bye-bye (bī'bī') interj. 1. Farewell. 2. "If I had my druthers, I'd be leaving right now." 3. "The pet is dead, but that is of no concern to me."

C choo-choo (choo'choo') n. 1. Train. 2. Father.

cookie (kŏŏk'ē) n. 1. A small, flat cake made with sugar and dough. See yum-yum.

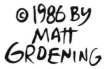

WHY MUST YOU ACT SO INFANTILE?

ICE

D dada (dä'dä') n. 1. Father. 2. Behemoth. 3. Any monster. 4. A European artistic and literary movement (1916-23) based on deliberate irrationality, chance, intuition, and comic derision.

doo-doo (doo'doo') n. 1. Excrement. 2. Anything taboo and unpleasant. 3. Anything taboo and exciting.

E eeee (ē) interj. 1. "Oh joy!" 2. "Help!" 3. "I could scream all day!"

F feh (fĕ) interj. 1. "Take it away; I am unamused."

G ga-ga (gä'gä') interj. 1. Look! 2. Wow! 3. Holy hop toads! 4. Gadzooks!

H hi (hī) interj. 1. Hello! 2. I exist! 3. Look at me, damn you!

I ick (ĭk) n. 1. Strained vegetables. 2. Excrement.

J jammies (jă'mēz) n. 1. Pyjamas. 2. Affectionate nickname of novelist Henry James.

L leggo (lĕ'pō) interj. 1. "Give me that object [toy, pacifier, knife, insecticide, etc.] right now! I need it!"

M mama (mä'ma) n. 1. Mother. 2. Any woman. 3. Babysitter. 4. Dog. 5. TV.

N no (nō) interj. 1. "I refuse!" 2. "I will not be budged!" 3. "I disagree with you vehemently!" 4. "I will not eat this slop!"

num-num (nŭm'nŭm') n. 1. Delicious food. 2. "Exquisite meal; I must get the recipe from you sometime."

O oh (ō) interj. 1. "I understand!" 2. "I am surprised!" 3. "Thank you for this toy; leave me alone now."

P pay-pen (pā'pĕn) n. 1. Playpen. 2. Prison.

pee-pee (pē'pē') n. 1. Tinkle. 2. Dinkle. 3. Wee-wee.

peez (pēz) interj. 1. Please. 2. I beg you. 3. "Do as I say or I will screech for as long as it takes."

LIFE IN HELL

© 1991 BY MATT GROENING

CALLING ALL CAFFEINE-ADDICTED MANIC-DEPRESSIVE CREATIVE TYPES!
GET OUT OF YOUR RATTY LITTLE APARTMENT AND LOITER SULLENLY AT

Akbar & Jeff's COFFEE HUT

FORMERLY AKBAR & JEFF'S FROZEN YOGURT HUT

OLDSTER BEATNIK SENIOR CITIZENS WELCOME IF YOU PROMISE NOT TO TELL US STORIES

"SERVING THE ALIENATED YOUNG RECOVERING ALCOHOLIC COMMUNITY SINCE 1990"

5% DISCOUNT IF YOU ARE ATTIRED SOLELY IN BLACK AND ARE WEARING SUNGLASSES AFTER DARK

- NO SHOES
- NO SHIRT
- NO NUKES

SCHEDULE

Mondays
ATONAL HOOTENANNY NITE If you like the sounds of industrial grinders you won't want to miss these young pioneers. A solemn time is guaranteed for all.

Wednesdays
TREASURES OF FRENCH SILENT AVANT-GARDE CINEMA The finest in scratchy 16mm 5th-generation duped prints will be shown on the far wall above the communal mural.

Thursdays
GIRLFRIENDS OF BITTER UNRECOGNIZED GENIUSES SUPPORT GROUP MEETING

I SURVIVED OPEN MIKE POETRY NITE AT AKBAR & JEFF'S COFFEE HUT

SOUVENIR MUGS $5 WITH PURCHASE OF LARGE BEVERAGE AND PASTRY PLATTER

Fridays
MYSTERY CELEBRITY NITE Each week we present a reading by another legendary award-winning 1950s-era beat misogynist poet

Saturdays
PERFORMANCE ART NITE The management cautions you not to eat any substance thrown, thrusted, or proffered by the performers, no matter how edible-looking.

Sundays
OPEN MIKE POETRY NITE The action is nonstop in this literary free-for-all. Bring your poems, lyrics, manifestoes, dream journals, suicide notes -- and let the fun begin!

VISIT OUR POETRY BOOKSTORE ON THE PREMISES IN THE NOOK IN THE FAR CORNER! SPECIAL GET-ACQUAINTED SALE! ALL BOOKS ON SALE 10¢ A DOZEN! NO RETURNS.

"THE MANAGEMENT CANNOT ACCEPT RESPONSIBILITY FOR SERVING YOU REGULAR WHEN YOU ORDERED DECAF."

LIFE IN HELL

©1990 BY MATT GROENING

UGH-- SO MANY POSEURS.

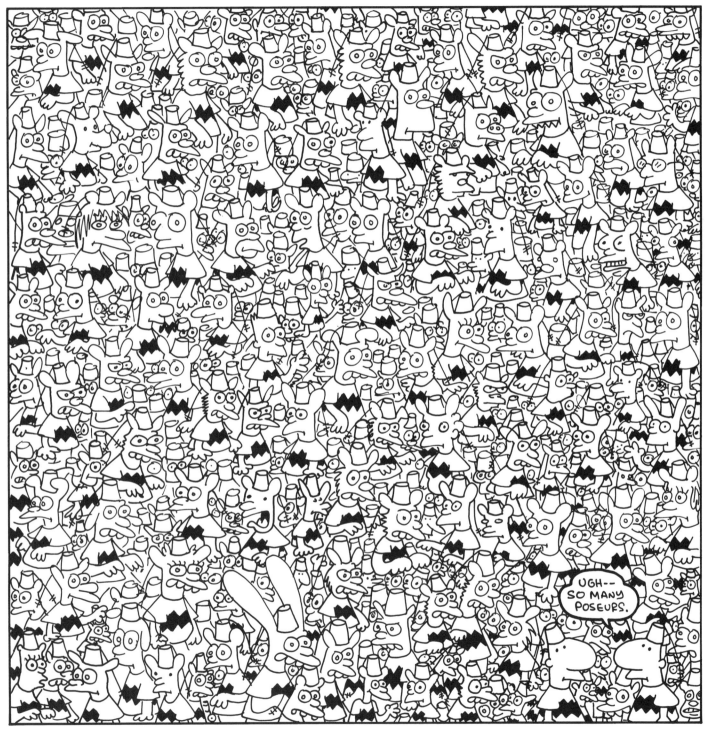

LIFE IN HELL

©1987 BY MATT GROENING

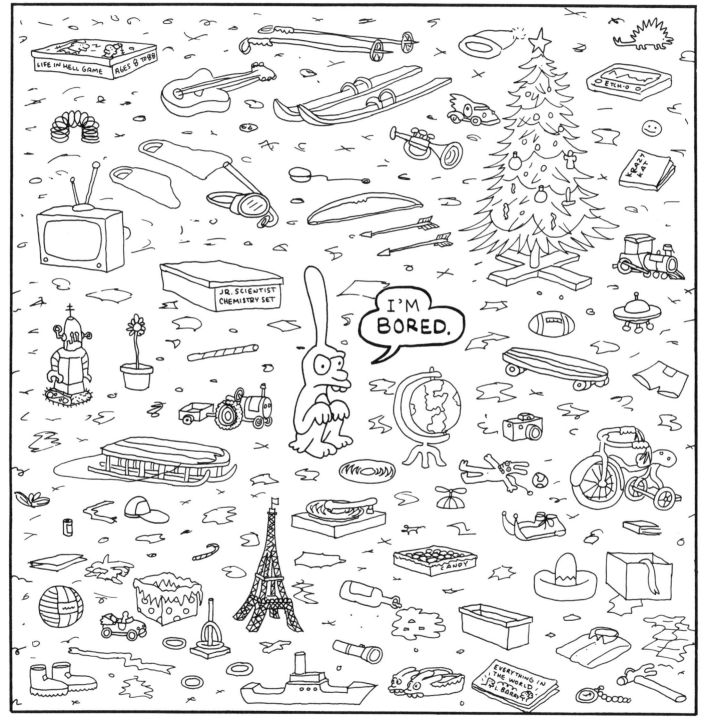

©1985 BY MATT GROENING

OFFICE SUPPLIES FROM HELL

PERMANENTLY STAINED

CHIPPED

ONLY 27 YEARS TILL RETIREMENT

WITTY COFFEE MUG

DRIED-UP BOTTLE OF CORRECTION FLUID

RATTLES WHEN YOU SHAKE IT

TYPO-B-GONE

LEAKS

MYSTERIOUS TOOTH MARKS (NOT YOUR OWN)

CHEAPEST BALLPOINT PEN ON EARTH

DECORATIVE WALL CALENDAR FEATURING AMUSING MISERABLE CHIMPS WITH SKIN DISEASES CAVORTING IN BUSINESS SUITS

SEPTEMBER 1985

PAPER CLIPS BENT INTO WEIRD SHAPES

SMELLY COFFEE POT WITH BROWN SLUDGE ON THE BOTTOM

OFFICE SUPPLIES FROM HELL

INEFFECTIVE BREATH MINTS

ASSORTED ERASER NUBBINS

FLICKERING FLUORESCENT LIGHTING

NO TALKING

MOTIVATIONAL PLAQUE

DEPRESSING CARTOON PINNED TO BULLETIN BOARD

DANISH WITH CHEMICAL AFTERTASTE

IDI INHUMAN DRUDGERY, INC.

6-66 / 66-6 NO. 09696

DATE 10/01/85

AMOUNT 75.00

PAY TO THE ORDER OF BINKY X

The Boss

LAUGHABLE PAYCHECK

HELL BIZ
©1984 BY MATT GROENING
STOREFRONT OF DOOM
Cafe Bongo
POETRY NITE TUES.
HOOTE-NANNY TONITE
BIG ED'S SLOT CAR RACING PALACE
NO GUM
NO LOITERING
REGIONAL YO-YO CHAMPIONSHIP HERE SAT.
PSYCHEDELIC HUT
CANDLES
BLACK LIGHT POSTERS
HEADBANDS
INCENSE
COMIX
IMPEACH GOV. REAGAN
MORT'S 8-TRACK QUAD TAPE EMPORIUM
WIN A WATERBED!
SALE!
"EXPERIENCE THE FULL MELLOW SOUNDS OF THE 70s"
Z.E.S.T. ZEAL ENRICHMENT SELF HOOD TRAINING
ABSOLUTELY NO REFUNDS
HOUSE OF SMILEYS
HAVE A NICE DAY!
SMILEY BUTTONS
SMILEY TOWELS
SMILEY T-SHIRTS
+ MORE!
NEW! RAINBOW 'N' UNICORN DECALS
PUNKY'S PUNK SHOP!
MOM N DAD GO HOME
PUNKS NOT DEAD
SID LIVES
GOLDIE'S TOAST-O-RAMA® TANNING SALON
AS SEEN ON TV!
LOOK HEALTHY! FOOL YOUR FRIENDS!
BREAKDANCING LESSONS
AS SEEN ON TV!
GRAFFITI ART SHOW IN OUR GALLERY
ANYONE BUT REAGAN

©1983 BY MATT GROENING

★ ANOTHER SELF-HELP NEWSPAPER CLIPPING TO TAPE TO YOUR FRIDGE AND IGNORE ★

HELLO, PORKUMS! HAD IT UP TO HERE [SLASHING GESTURE TOWARDS THROBBING BELLY] WITH ALL THEM CRUMMY DIETS THAT TREAT YOU LIKE A SLOW-WITTED CREAMPUFF IN THEIR OPTIMISTIC BREEZINESS?
WELL THEN, CHUBS, LOOKS LIKE YOUR READY FOR

PREVENTATIVE SNACK FRENZY®

YUMMY CANDY LETTERS

CAN YOU FIND THE SECRET FUDGE BITS?

① PILE ALL TEMPTATIONS ON THE TABLE AROUND MIDNIGHT TONIGHT. IT'S SHOWDOWN TIME IN OINKVILLE, U.S.A.

FRIJ — WARM FRENZY

LEFTOVER KUNG PAO CHICKEN

DEVIL'S FOOD CAKE [DETAIL]

MARINATED ARTICHOKE HEARTS

HEFTY ROAST BEEF SAMWICH

LOBSTER BISQUE

COLD BROCCOLI (OPTIONAL)

PYRAMID OF FROSTED DONUTS

EXOTIC BEVERAGE FROM ABROAD
LOCO JUICE

ICE CREAM WITH SECRET FUDGE BITS

PASTE PHOTO OF YOUR FAVORITE SNACK HERE

THERE IS NO FREE WILL.

WHATS FER DINNER?

② PICTURE ALL THEM OTHER DIETS YOU BEEN ON THAT HAVE FAILED YOU MISERABLY, LEAVING YOU BEACHED LIKE A POOR LI'L BLEATING BABY WALRUS.

TUB — 15 CALORIES

DIE COL WITH METALLIC AFTER-TASTE!

THE 40 JUGS OF WATER A DIET
1 2 3

I ♥ SELF-INDUCED VOMITING

PRANCEROBICS TEE HEE

MAKES YA HONGRY JES LOOKIN AT EM DONIT? WELL, FORGET EM!

③ NOW WE COME TO THE SECRET FORMULA OF PREVENTATIVE SNACK FRENZY® -- PRETENDING YOUR MOST FAVORITE YUM-TREATS ARE ACTUALLY CRAWLING WITH VERMIN! YOU'LL LOSE YOUR APPETITE IMMEDIATELY, AND IF YOU CONCENTRATE CREATIVELY, IT CAN ACTUALLY BE A FUN MEALTIME GAME.

THIS   BECOMES THIS

FRIED DRUMSTICK   SLIMY GARDEN SLUG

BOWL O' CEREAL   BOWL O' WEEVILS

DONUT   MUD EEL

④ SIMPLE, ISN'T IT? ALL YOU GOTTA DO IS LOOK DOWN AND THINK REVOLTING THOUGHTS! IT'S EASY!

HEY Y'KNOW THESE STINKBEETLE GRUBS AIN'T BAD ONCE YA GET USED TO 'EM.

HEAVY SYRUP

WHIPPED CREAM

TUB OF ICE CREAM

THE BIG PICTURE

I'M GOING TO TELL GOD TO STAB YOU.

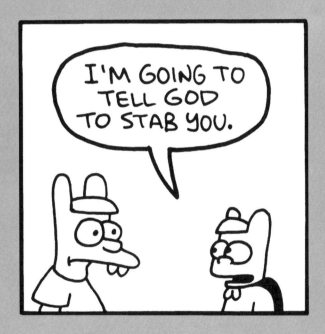

LIFE IN HELL
©1995 BY MATT GROENING
OW!
QUIT PUNCHIN' ME!
WELL, YOU MAKE ME MAD SOMETIMES, ABE.
I'M GOING TO TELL GOD TO STAB YOU.
WHAT???
THAT'S IMPOSSIBLE.
GOD ISN'T A HUMAN, YOU KNOW.
I KNOW.
SO GOD DOESN'T HAVE HANDS.
I KNOW.
WELL, IF GOD DOESN'T HAVE HANDS, THAT MEANS HE CAN'T HOLD A KNIFE.
OH.
AND IF GOD CAN'T HOLD A KNIFE, HOW CAN GOD STAB ME?
WELL...
I'M GOING TO TELL GOD TO KICK YOU.

LIFE IN HELL

©1995 BY MATT GROENING

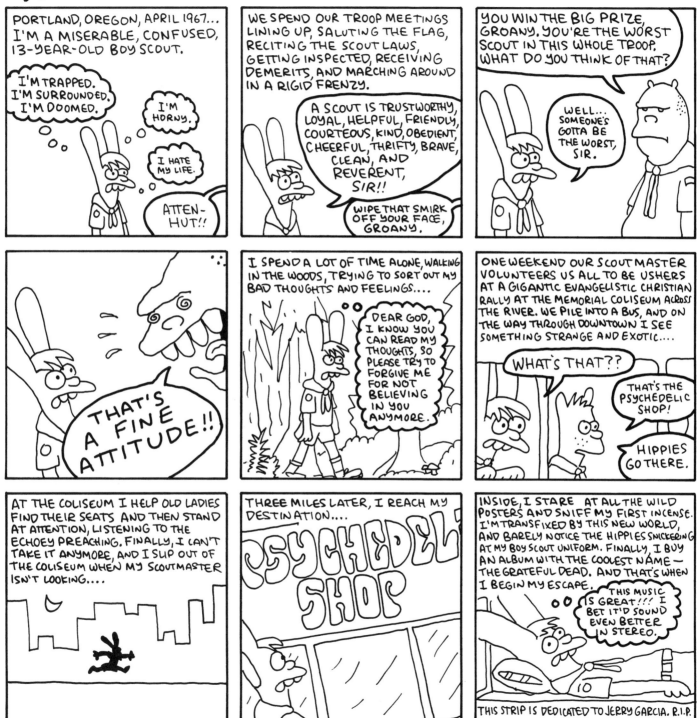

THIS STRIP IS DEDICATED TO JERRY GARCIA. R.I.P.

LIFE IN HELL
©1994 BY MATT GROENING
I JUST STUBBED MY TOE. IT REALLY HURTS.
THAT'S A BUMMER. MAYBE I CAN EASE THE PAIN.
BASICALLY, LIFE IS A HOPELESS, FUTILE STRUGGLE.
WE JUST WASTE OUR LIMITED TIME ON EARTH PRETENDING WHAT WE DO HAS ANY SIGNIFICANCE AT ALL.
WE DON'T WANT TO ADMIT IT, BUT EVERYTHING IS POINTLESS.
FROM THE MOMENT WE'RE CONCEIVED, WE'RE ON A STEADY DOWNHILL SLIDE TO TOTAL ANNIHILATION.
OUR GOOSE IS COOKED, MAN.
THAT'S SUPPOSED TO EASE MY PAIN?
YOU FORGOT ABOUT YOUR STUPID STUBBED TOE, DIDN'T YOU?

LIFE IN HELL
©1994 BY MATT GROENING
MATT! COME HERE! I HAVE TO ASK YOU SOMETHING.
WHAT IS THE SOUL?
UH, WELL... THAT'S A TOUGH ONE....
THE SOUL IS SORT OF LIKE, YOU KNOW, YOUR INNER SPIRIT....
IT'S THE BEST PART OF YOU... UH... INSIDE YOU... THIS THING....
IT'S THIS... DEEP... YOUR DEEPEST... FEELINGS.... YOUR HEART... IN YOU....
IT'S, UH... IT'S YOUR LIFE FORCE, UH... YEAH, THAT'S IT.
THEN WHY DO THE SEA ZOMBIES GIVE UP THEIR SOULS TO SKULLMASTER???

LIFE IN HELL
©1990 BY MATT GROENING
I CAN'T SLEEP AT NIGHT BECAUSE I WORRY ABOUT THE FINALITY OF DEATH.
DEATH ISN'T FINAL.
I THINK WE'RE ALL PART OF A BIG COSMIC REPEATING CYCLE THAT WE DON'T FULLY UNDERSTAND.
LIFE HAPPENS ONCE-- WHY NOT AGAIN? I BELIEVE THAT WE REPEAT OUR LIVES INFINITE NUMBERS OF TIMES, EXACTLY THE SAME EACH TIME.
THINK ABOUT IT.
YIKES.

LIFE IN HELL
©1989 BY MATT GROENING
HOW LONG WILL YOU LIVE?
A FUN TEST
START THIS FUN TEST WITH 73 LUCKY BONUS POINTS.
IF YOU ARE FEMALE, ADD 4.
IF MALE, SUBTRACT 5.
IF YOU LIVE ON A SMALL ISLAND IN THE SOUTH PACIFIC ALL BY YOURSELF, ADD 3.
IF YOU LIVE IN A SMALL APARTMENT IN A LARGE CITY WITH A ROOMMATE WHO WHISTLES, SUBTRACT 4.
IF ANY GRANDPARENT LIVED TO BE 93, ADD 2.
IF YOU HAD TO ATTEND ANY GRANDPARENT'S OPEN-CASKET FUNERAL, SUBTRACT 2.
IF YOU WORK BEHIND A DESK, SUBTRACT 2.
IF YOUR WORK REQUIRES LIFTING DESKS, SUBTRACT 3.
IF YOU WORK WITH COMPUTERS, SUBTRACT 2.
IF YOU DREAM ABOUT COMPUTERS, SUBTRACT 3.
IF YOU WORK ON A CATWALK ABOVE HUGE VATS OF NOXIOUS BOILING LIQUIDS, SUBTRACT 5.
IF YOU DRINK COFFEE, SUBTRACT 1.
DECAF IS HELL
IF YOU ARE ANNOYED BY THE PHRASE "HAVE A NICE DAY," SUBTRACT 3.
IF YOU HAVE EATEN A DONUT IN THE LAST 10 YEARS, SUBTRACT 4.
IF YOU HAVE EVER EVEN THOUGHT ABOUT GOING TO GRADUATE SCHOOL, SUBTRACT 2.
IF YOU GET INTO LOUD ARGUMENTS WITH STRANGERS ON BUSES, SUBTRACT 2.
I ♥ NY
IF YOU LIVE WITH A SPOUSE OR FRIEND, ADD 2.
IF THE SPOUSE OR FRIEND IS A POET, SUBTRACT 3.
IF YOU HAVE EVER WORN LEATHER PANTS, SUBTRACT 2.
IF YOU HAVE EVER DATED SOMEONE WHO WORE LEATHER PANTS, SUBTRACT 1.
YOO HOO.
IF YOU WEAR SUNGLASSES AT NIGHT, SUBTRACT 3.
IF YOU ARE IMPRESSED BY ROCK STARS WHO POUT, SUBTRACT 2.
IF YOU ARE IMPRESSED BY PERFORMANCE ARTISTS WHO PELT YOU WITH MEAT BY-PRODUCTS, SUBTRACT 3.
ARE YOU ANGRY AND VINDICTIVE, OR FROM NEW YORK? SUBTRACT 2.
ARE YOU RELAXED AND MELLOW? SUBTRACT 2.
ARE YOU HIP AND SELF-SATISFIED, OR FROM LOS ANGELES? SUBTRACT 3.
IF YOU RESENT THIS TEST, SUBTRACT 3.
VOILÀ!!
YOUR SCORE AT THIS POINT IS YOUR LIFE EXPECTANCY.
Have a nice day.

LIFE IN HELL
©1989 BY MATT GROENING (WITH SAM SIMON)
WHAT DO YOU WANT ON YOUR TOMBSTONE?
37 YEARS IN THERAPY "ALMOST CURED"
AMASSED A MOST IMPRESSIVE CD COLLECTION
I PLAN TO WIN THE LOTTERY IN MY NEXT LIFE
LIVED SLOW, DIED YOUNG, SURE WISH I'D LIVED FAST
NEVER VOTED FOR A WINNER IN A MAJOR ELECTION
WOULD YOU MIND READING MY SCREENPLAY?
BOUGHT THE SATANIC VERSES, A BRIEF HISTORY OF TIME, AND THE ANDY WARHOL DIARIES, BUT NEVER GOT AROUND TO READING 'EM
I DON'T DECAY IN YOUR LAWN. PLEASE DON'T WALK ON MY GRAVE.
HERE LIES "OL' BLACK TONGUE" WROTE FRIVOLOUS CARTOON STRIP FOR 23 YEARS ONLY TO DIE OF INK POISONING AFTER SUCKING ON ONE TOO MANY CLOGGED PENS

©1984 BY MATT GROENING

WHAT DID YOU AMOUNT TO?

A HANDY POCKET-SIZED SCORECARD FOR YOU TO FILL OUT ON YOUR DEATH-BED SO YOU CAN PASS ON TO THE NEXT WORLD—OR WHATEVER— WITH THE FULL—IF NOT LASTING—SATISFACTION OF KNOWING—AT LEAST FOR A FEW FINAL FLEETING MOMENTS—YOUR TRUE, UTTER, ABSOLUTE, TOTAL WORTH. CHEATERS WILL BE SEVERELY PUNISHED.

INFANCY

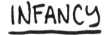

FIRST WORDS:
- [ ] "DA-DA" [1 PT.]
- [ ] "MA-MA" [1 PT.]
- [ ] "SAY, THIS IS DELICIOUS." [9 PTS.]

AWARDS AND CERTIFICATES

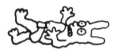

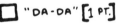

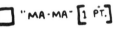

- [ ] HALL MONITOR BADGE [1 PT.]
- [ ] HIGH SCHOOL DIPLOMA [1 PT.]
- [ ] COLLEGE DIPLOMA [1 PT.; -2 PTS. FOR DEGREE IN ENGLISH OR PHILOSOPHY]
- [ ] ACADEMY AWARD ("OSCAR") [1 PT. IF ACCEPTANCE SPEECH IS LESS THAN 25 SECONDS; -2 PTS. PER SECOND THEREAFTER]

RELIGION

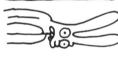

AGE AT WHICH YOU REALIZED YOUR RELIGIOUS UPBRINGING WAS BALONEY:
- [ ] 10 YRS. [5 PTS.]
- [ ] 12 YRS. [4 PTS.]
- [ ] 15 YRS. [3 PTS.]
- [ ] 18 YRS. [2 PTS.]
- [ ] 40 YRS. [-8 PTS.]

RESPONSIBILITY

- [ ] # OF TIMES YOU VOTED FOR A DEMOCRAT [1 PT EA.] OR A REPUBLICAN [-4 PTS EA.]
- [ ] # OF NIGHTS YOU SLEPT SOUNDLY WHILE OTHERS IN THE WORLD SUFFERED UNDER THE OPPRESSION OF U.S.-SUPPORTED RIGHT-WING REGIMES [-3 PTS. EA.]

WEIGHT

- [ ] # OF ABANDONED DIETS [-3 PTS. EA.]
- [ ] # OF VILE-TASTING DIET BEVERAGES DRUNK [-1 PT. EA. GAL.]
- [ ] # OF DONUTS EATEN TO GET RID OF VILE TASTE OF DIET BEVERAGE IN MOUTH [-1 PT. EA. FROSTED DONUT; -2 PTS. EA. FROSTED DONUT WITH COLORED SPRINKLES]

TATTOOS

- [ ] NONE [1 PT.]
- [ ] "BORN TO RAISE HELL" [1 PT.]
- [ ] ANY MISSPELLED WORDS [-1 PT. EA.]

AMOUR

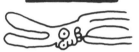

- [ ] # OF MEANINGFUL RELATIONSHIPS [1 PT. EA.]
- [ ] # OF MEANINGFUL RELATIONSHIPS WITH SCREAMING ARGUMENTS [-2 PTS. EA.]
- [ ] # OF FROSTED DONUTS EATEN WHEN HEART-BROKEN [-1 PT. EA.]

YOUR FINAL SCORE

-50 TO 0 POINTS: YOU OUGHT TO BE ASHAMED OF YOURSELF.

1 TO 25 POINTS: YOU OUGHT TO BE ASHAMED OF YOURSELF.

26 POINTS AND UP: YOU HAVE NO SHAME.

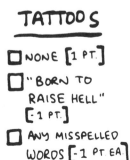

NB DO NOT LEAVE THIS SCORECARD IN COAT POCKET. IT COULD VERY WELL END UP IN SOME MUSTY THRIFT SHOP ALONG WITH THE REST OF YOUR STUFF.

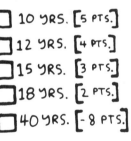

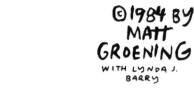

LEFTOVERS
IN HELL

SON OF
WHAT WILL THEY WRITE ON YOUR TOMBSTONE?

THIS LITTLE SNEAK NEVER DID THE DISHES WHEN IT WAS HIS TURN

HOPED TO DIRECT SOMEDAY

NICE TRY

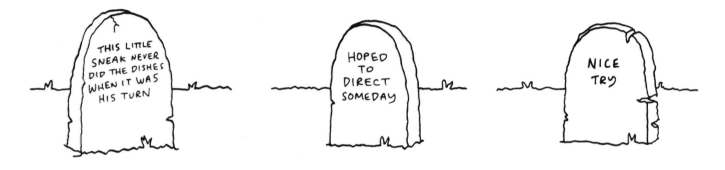

THEY CALLED HER "PIXIE BUTT" BEHIND HER BACK

LOUSY TIPPER

I HELPED INVADE NICARAGUA AND ALL I GOT WAS THIS LOUSY TOMBSTONE

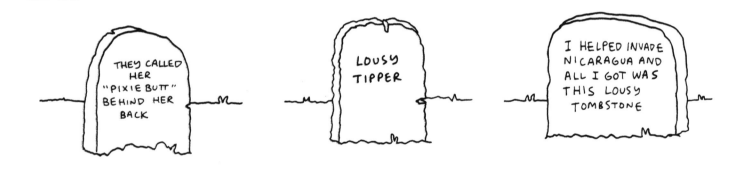

WENT TO MEXICO ONCE; DIDN'T LIKE IT "FOOD TOO SPICY"

I'M WITH STUPID

FINALLY

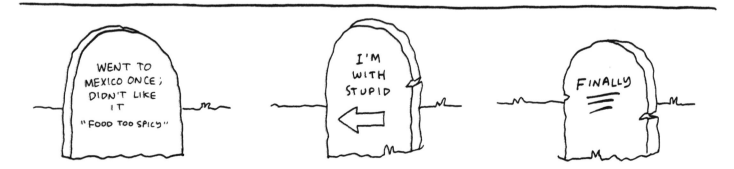

LIFE IN HELL
©1995 BY MATT GROENING
IF WE'RE GOING TO BE TOGETHER FOR THE REST OF OUR LIVES, THAT MEANS EVENTUALLY ONE OF US IS GOING TO OUTLIVE THE OTHER.
WE SHOULD PLAN THE KINDS OF FUNERALS WE WANT.
WELL, THIS MAY SEEM WEIRD, BUT I'VE GOT A FANTASY FUNERAL ALREADY IN MY HEAD.
I ENVISION A GRAND AFFAIR.
IN HAWAII. FLY IN FRIENDS FROM ALL OVER.
QUICK CREMATION, THEN SCATTER THE ASHES IN A VOLCANO.
THEN, THAT NIGHT, A GIANT LUAU.
ROAST PIG ON THE BEACH. LIMBO CONTESTS. LOTS OF BEER.
THREE BANDS: REGGAE, ZYDECO, AND BLUES.
SWIMMING IN THE MOONLIGHT. NAKED DANCING AT MIDNIGHT.
A TOTALLY DECADENT CELEBRATION.
WHAT DO YOU THINK?
WELL, GEE, I ALWAYS THOUGHT A FUNERAL WOULD BE THE TIME FOR A QUIET REFLECTION IN GRIEF AND SORROW.
I'M AMAZED YOU WANT YOUR FUNERAL TO BE A PARTY.
I WAS TALKING ABOUT **YOUR** FUNERAL.

LIFE IN HELL
©1996 BY MATT GROENING
WE'RE TRAPPED IN A VICIOUS CYCLE HERE.
WHAT DO YOU MEAN?
I MEAN A SITUATION IN WHICH THE EFFORT TO SOLVE A PROBLEM ONLY RESULTS IN THE AGGRAVATION OF THE PROBLEM, OR CREATES A NEW, EVEN WORSE PROBLEM.
YOU MEAN THE MORE WE TRY TO MAKE THINGS BETTER, THE WORSE WE END UP FEELING?
EXACTLY! EVEN THOUGH WE BOTH WANT TO BE LOVED, APPRECIATED, AND UNDERSTOOD.
IT'S A BEAUTIFUL THING TO BE ABLE TO COMMUNICATE OPENLY AND WITHOUT FEAR. I... I LOVE YOU.
AND I... I LOVE YOU.
WOW.
SO MUCH FOR BEING TRAPPED IN AN ENDLESS CYCLE OF RESENTMENT AND NEGATIVITY!
BY THE WAY, THE TERM IS "VICIOUS CIRCLE," NOT "VICIOUS CYCLE," STUPID.

THE LEARNING EXPERIENCE

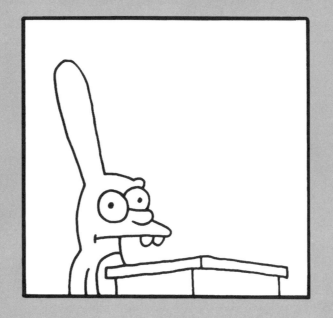

LIFE IN HELL
©1995 BY MATT GROENING
ALL RIGHT, STUDENTS! WHO IS GOING TO VOLUNTEER TO LEAD TODAY'S VOLUNTARY, STUDENT-LED PRAYER?
ANYONE?
OK, BONGO!
DEAR LORD, LET US PRAY THAT SOMEDAY THE SUPREME COURT WILL NOT BE PACKED WITH RIGHT-WING CREEPS, AND THAT THE SEPARATION OF CHURCH AND STATE WILL ONCE AGAIN BE UPHELD, AND THAT WE CAN GET THE PUBLIC SCHOOLS OUT OF THE RELIGION BUSINESS AND BACK TO EDUCATION. AMEN.

LIFE IN HELL

THERE! DON'T YOU FEEL LESS VIOLENT IN YOUR NEW SCHOOL UNIFORM?

LIFE IN HELL
©1994 BY MATT GROENING
GOOD NEWS, EVERYONE! WE'VE GOT PRAYER IN THE SCHOOL!! ALL JEWS, ATHEISTS, HINDUS, MUSLIMS, SHINTOISTS, TAOISTS, SUFIS, BUDDHISTS, AND OTHER HEATHENS SHOULD LEAVE THE ROOM NOW.

LIFE IN HELL
©1990 BY MATT GROENING
WHERE IS YOUR HOMEWORK, BONGO?
HOW WILL I LOOK BACK ON THIS MOMENT TWENTY YEARS FROM NOW?
PERHAPS WITH A SMALL SHUDDER OF REGRET.
I HAD SOMETHING TO OFFER, YET I SQUANDERED MY MEAGER TALENTS.
I HAD YOUTH AND HEALTH AND POSSIBILITY, YET I RISKED SO LITTLE.
I LET THE MOMENT DRIFT BY UNNOTICED, CARRYING ME CLOSER TO MY GRAVE.
I REMAINED ABSORBED BY MEANINGLESS TRIVIA AND RELENTLESS ROUTINE.
I COULDN'T PLAN WELL AND I FORGOT THE PLANS I DID MAKE.
MY LIFE WAS A MUDDLE OF POINTLESS TASKS, BRAINLESS IMPULSES, AND VIGOROUS DENIALS.
I HAD NO COHERENT GOALS OF ANY KIND.
I WAS LOST IN TIME, UNAWARE OF THE URGENCY OF EACH FLEETING SECOND.
I POSTPONED MY OWN LIFE WITH BARELY A SECOND THOUGHT.
BUT WAIT! BY THINKING THESE THOUGHTS, THERE'S STILL HOPE!
HOWEVER PAINFUL IT MAY BE, I AM SLOWLY BUT SURELY EDGING TOWARD ENLIGHTENMENT!
HELLO, FUTURE SELF! IT'S ME, YOUNG BONGO!! I AM HERE NOW, I AM AWARE, AND I AM ALIVE!
THE DOG ATE IT.

LIFE IN HELL
©1987 BY MATT GROENING WITH DEBORAH CAPLAN
THE SECRET OF CRYING CONVINCINGLY
Young Tattletale MAGAZINE
PRICE: 25¢ IN STOLEN MILK MONEY
NO. 1
ENTERTAINMENT FOR SQUEALERS
Our Motto:
I'M TELLING.
HOW TO DARE OTHERS TO BE NAUGHTY SO YOU CAN REPORT THEM LATER
FEIGNING INJURY TO GAIN SYMPATHY
SPECIAL FLEXIDISC ENCLOSED! "THE SQUEALER'S ANTHEM"
"NYAH-NAH NYAH-NAH NYAH-NYAH"
DOES CROSSING YOUR FINGERS BEHIND YOUR BACK WHILE YOU SAY "I SWEAR ON A STACK OF BIBLES" ALLOW YOU TO LIE? OUR EXPERTS SAY YES!
WHAT'S SO BAD ABOUT FEELING LIKE A GOODY-GOODY?
THE ULTIMATE SNITCH: TURNING IN YOUR PARENTS FOR DRUGS!!!

THE BATTLE HYMN OF HELL
©1984 BY MATT GROENING
MINE EYES HAVE SEEN THE GLORY OF THE BURNING OF THE SCHOOL
WE HAVE TORTURED ALL THE TEACHERS
WE HAVE BROKEN EVERY RULE
WE HAVE BARBECUED THE PRINCIPAL
DESTROYED THE PTA
US KIDS GO MARCHING ON.
GLORY, GLORY HALLELUJAH
TEACHER HIT ME WITH A RULER
SO I SHOT HER IN THE BUTT
WITH A ROTTEN COCONUT
AND SHE AIN'T NO TEACHER NO MORE.
MORNIN, MS. WHITE.

LIFE IN HELL
©1991 BY MATT GROENING
PLEASE RISE FOR THE FLAG SALUTE.
I PLEDGE IMPERTINENCE TO THE FLAG-WAVING
OF THE UNINDICTED CO-CONSPIRATORS OF AMERICA
AND TO THE REPUBLICANS FOR WHICH I CAN'T STAND
ONE ABOMINATION, UNDERHANDED FRAUD
INDEFENSIBLE
WITH LIBERTY AND JUSTICE FORGET IT.
HEH HEH
JUST KIDDING.

LIFE IN HELL
©1995 BY MATT GROENING
WHY DOES AMERICA HATE ITS KIDS?
OUR SCHOOLS ARE FALLING APART!
THE CLASSROOMS ARE OVERCROWDED AND THE TEACHERS ARE UNDERPAID!
WE HAVE TO LEARN FROM TEXTBOOKS CENSORED SO AS TO NOT OFFEND THE GRIMMEST RIGHT-WING CHRISTIAN SENSIBILITIES!
AND EDUCATIONAL FUNDING KEEPS GETTING CUT!
WHAT'S THE LOGIC BEHIND CUTTING SCHOOL BREAKFAST PROGRAMS FOR THE POOR, OR CUTTING AID TO KIDS WITH DISABILITIES?
KIDS ARE GOING TO GROW UP, YOU KNOW.
WHY AREN'T WE PLANNING FOR THE FUTURE??
DON'T WORRY. BY THE TIME YOU AND YOUR LITTLE BUDDIES DROP OUT OF HIGH SCHOOL, WE'LL HAVE YOUR PRISON CELLS BUILT AND READY TO GO.

©1987 BY MATT GROENING

BACK PAIN IN HELL

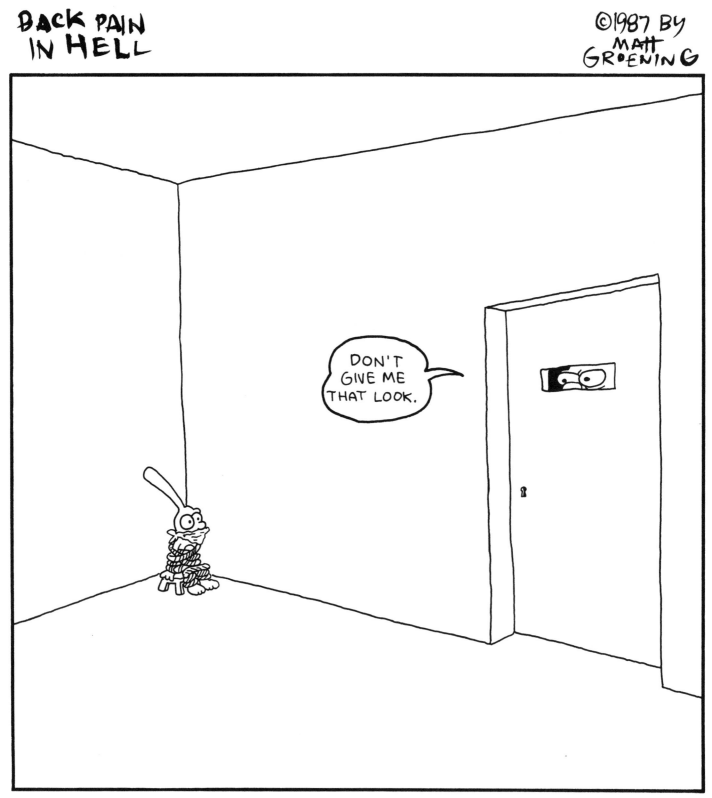

ENLIGHTENMENT IS HELL

LIFE IN HELL
©1989 BY MATT GROENING
KIDS WANT TO KNOW
DO DOG MOVIE-STARS KNOW THEY'RE FAMOUS?
WHAT DID PEOPLE DO AT NIGHT BEFORE THERE WAS TV?
DO ANTS HAVE SOULS?
WHAT DOES HUMAN FLESH TASTE LIKE?
WHAT IF THE OPPOSITE SEX ARE ALL REALLY MARTIANS?
WHO INVENTED THE IDEA OF STICKING YOUR GUM UNDER THE TABLE IN RESTAURANTS?
DON'T PLANTS GET BORED JUST SITTING THERE?
DO SLUGS DREAM?
DO CARS FEEL PAIN WHEN THEY CRASH?
WHAT IF EVERYONE IN THE WORLD IS A ROBOT EXCEPT ME?
ARE STARVING CHILDREN ON TV REALLY REAL?
IF CATS THOUGHT THEY COULD GET AWAY WITH IT, WOULD THEY MURDER US ALL IN OUR SLEEP?
DID PEOPLE IN THE OLD DAYS REALIZE HOW CORNY THEY WERE?
HOW DO YOU REALLY KNOW FOR SURE WHEN A QUESTION HAS BEEN ANSWERED?
WHY CAN'T I HAVE ANOTHER COOKIE?

©1989
BY MATT
GROENING

raeD yraiD, I thguoht
tuoba xes yadot.

LIFE IN HELL
©1988 BY MATT GROENING
CHILDHOOD FAVORITES REVISITED
THE LITTLE ENGINE WHO COULD STOP DRINKING ANYTIME HE WANTED TO, ONLY HE DIDN'T WANT TO
LITTLE RED RIDING HOOD AND THE BIG BAD WOODSMAN SHE MARRIED
ALICE OUT OF WONDERLAND AND IN AND OUT OF INSTITUTIONS
THE DAUGHTER WHO TURNED INTO HER MOTHER
THE UGLY DUCKLING WHO GREW UP TO BE A BEAUTIFUL SWAN AND THEN MADE INCESSANT ANTI-UGLY-DUCKLING REMARKS
SNOW WHITE AND THE SEVEN SHORT NEEDY BOYFRIENDS
THE BOY WHO CRIED WOLF BUT WHO STOPPED AFTER ELECTROSHOCK TREATMENTS
THE LITTLE ENGINE WHO COULD, EXCEPT HE ATE FATTY FOODS AND DIED OF HEART DISEASE
THE SON WHO TURNED INTO HIS FATHER
SLEEPING BEAUTY AND HER LIFELONG DROWSINESS AND DEPRESSION
THE PARENTS WHO DID TO THEIR CHILDREN WHAT THEIR PARENTS HAD DONE TO THEM
GOOD GRIEF, IT'S LIFE IN HELL

LIFE IN HELL

©1986 BY MATT GROENING
CHICAGO

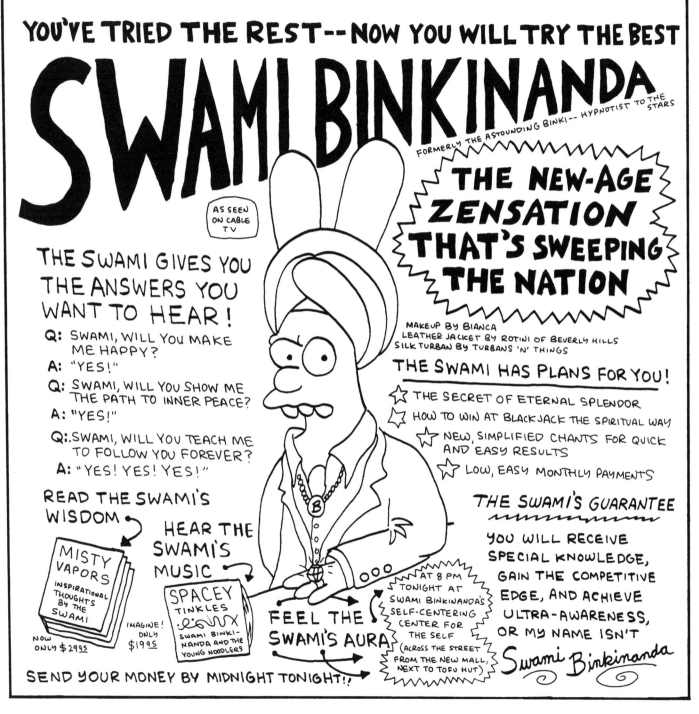

119

LIFE IN HELL

©1986 BY MATT GROENING

THE DECENT PERSON'S GUIDE TO PORN, SLIME, & FILTH

		ALSO KNOWN AS	CHARACTERISTICS	AUDIENCE	PURPOSE	DEGRADES	REACTION BY ANTI-PORN CRUSADERS	REACTION BY PORN CUSTOMERS	REACTION BY SEXUALLY ACTIVE YOUNGFOLK
FAMILY FARE		WHOLESOME ENTERTAINMENT, FUN FOR YOUNG AND OLD	VIOLENCE, DEATH, CORNY JOKES	REPUBLICANS, CHILDREN, SLOW ADULTS	ENTERTAINMENT	INTELLIGENCE	LOVE IT!	VERY BORED	NOT INTERESTED
TRASH		GARBAGE, RUBBISH, ART	LOUD, VULGAR, BAD JOKES	TEENAGERS, EX-TEENAGERS	HELPS TO DISTRACT FROM THE MEANINGLESSNESS OF ONE'S IMPENDING DEATH	INTELLIGENCE	HATE IT!	BORED	OCCASIONALLY INTERESTED
EROTICA		RIBALDRY BAWDY STUFF, ART	GENTLE, SOFT-FOCUS, SILLY	BORED COUPLES, MASTURBATORS	FANTASIES, FOREPLAY, MASTURBATION, LAUGHS	INTELLIGENCE	REALLY HATE IT!	BORED	BASICALLY NOT INTERESTED
SMUT		FOULNESS, VULGARITY, ART	SAME AS TRASH, ONLY DIRTIER	MASTURBATORS, THE CURIOUS	MASTURBATION, LAUGHS	INTELLIGENCE	LOATHE IT!	INTRIGUED	NOT INTERESTED
SLEAZE		DEFILEMENT, SWILL, ART	SAME AS SMUT, ONLY WITH WORSE JOKES	MASTURBATORS, THE CURIOUS	MASTURBATION, LAUGHS	INTELLIGENCE	DESPISE IT!	EXCITED	NOT INTERESTED
PORN		SCUM, DEBASEMENT, ART	SAME AS SLEAZE, ONLY WITH EVEN WORSE JOKES	MASTURBATORS, THE CURIOUS	MASTURBATION, LAUGHS	INTELLIGENCE	WANT TO KILL IT!	YEAH!	NOT INTERESTED
SLIME		SCUZZ, DIRT, ART	SAME AS PORN, ONLY WITH SCARIER PERFORMERS	MASTURBATORS, THE CURIOUS	MASTURBATION, LAUGHS	INTELLIGENCE	WANT TO STOMP IT, THEN KILL IT!	WOW!	NOT INTERESTED
FILTH		ALL OF THE ABOVE (EXCEPT FAMILY FARE)	SAME AS SLIME, EXCEPT FEATURING PERVERSIONS YOU NEVER THOUGHT OF BEFORE	CURIOUS MASTURBATORS	MASTURBATION	INTELLIGENCE	SAME AS ABOVE, ONLY SLOWER	OOH-WEE!!	NOT INTERESTED
ACTUAL SEX		JAZZING, MAKING LOVE, A ROLL IN THE HAY	REALLY FUN, GOOD JOKES (afterwards)	MOST EVERYONE EXCEPT A FEW CURIOUS MASTURBATORS	FUN, LOVE, LAUGHS	THAT ALL DEPENDS	LOVE THE IDEA OF FORNICATORS WRITHING IN THE EVERLASTING FLAMES OF HELL	IF WE HAD THIS, WE WOULDN'T NEED PORN	LOVE IT!

LIFE IN HELL

SCHOOL PSYCHIATRIST
NUNNA YER BEESWAX.

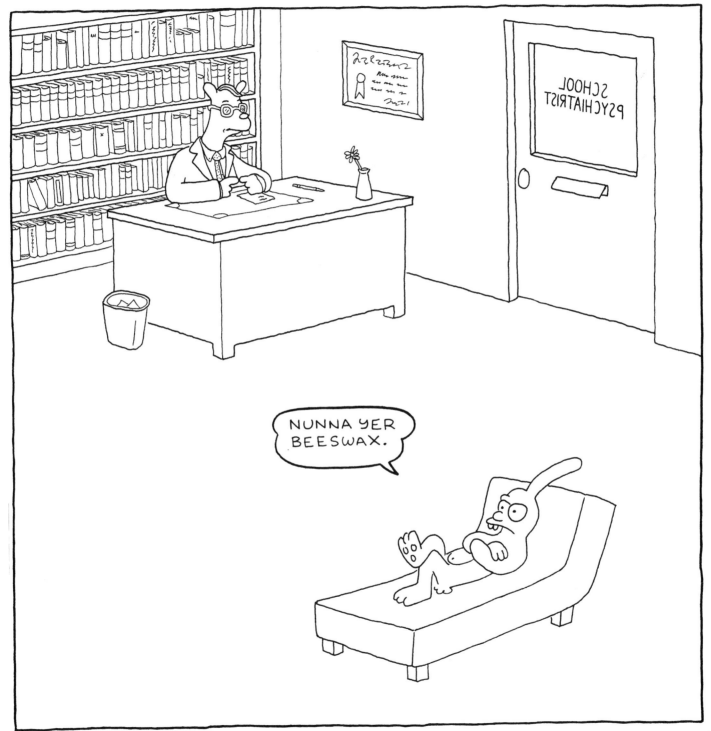

HOT AS
HELL

©1984
BY MATT
GROENING

QUESTIONABLE SWAMIS

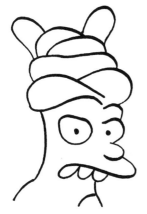

SWAMI JEFF

"A JOURNEY OF A THOUSAND
MILES BEGINS WITH BUT A
SINGLE GENEROUS DONATION."

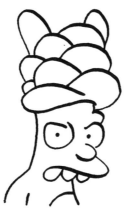

SWAMI PETE

"YOUR SECRET MANTRA
IS 'MOO.'"

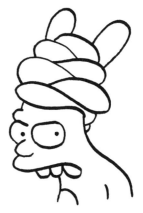

SWAMI BRAD

"SHUT YER TRAP AND
MEDITATE."

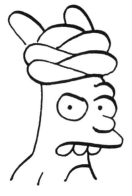

SWAMI JO-JO

"OPEN YOUR MOUTH AND CLOSE
YOUR EYES AND YOU WILL
GET A BIG SURPRISE."

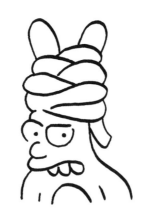

FROSTY THE SWAMI

"WHERE'S THE GODDAMN
MONEY?"

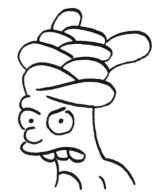

SWAMI BINKINANDA

"KISS MY ENLIGHTENED ASS."

LIFE IN HELL

GIVE ME ONE GOOD REASON I SHOULDN'T KILL MYSELF.
MMMM-- NEW FLAVOR.

LIFE IN HELL

EVERGREEN
SCREAMERS
STOP
HANG IN THERE, BABY
top secret
danger
keep out
ESQUIVEL
YMA SUMAC
VENUTI
MAMBO! with PEREZ PRADO
ROTA
LEE PERRY
EXOTICA
JIMBO
BENCHLE
THURBE
LARDNE
PERELMA
VONNEG
POGO
WODEHOU
LITTLE LULU
LI'L ABNER
SHUT UP, I'M MEDITATIN
UNCLE SCROOGE

LET'S DANCE

HI, HONEY, I'M--
ULP!

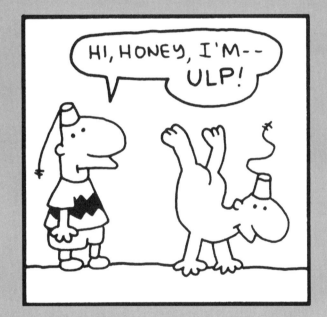

LIFE IN HELL
©1996 BY MATT GROENING
BOYS, BOYS, BOYS! DON'T YOU SEE WHAT YOU'RE DOING TO EACH OTHER? YOU'RE BOTH CAUGHT UP IN A DANCE -- A DANCE OF DESTRUCTION!
YOU WALTZ AROUND IN A RITUALIZED EXCHANGE OF SULKING RESENTMENT AND SIMMERING RAGE.
THEN YOU SLIP INTO A MAMBO OF MUTUAL MISUNDERSTANDING, PUNCTUATED BY PIROUETTES OF PROVOCATION.
WHICH LEADS INTO A BUNNYHOP OF BICKERING, BELITTLING, AND BLAME, FOLLOWED BY A RUMBA OF WRATH, RIGIDITY, AND REJECTION.
THEN YOU GO RIGHT INTO THE HOT-HEADED HULA OF HOSTILITY!
AND FROM THERE YOU END UP IN A SURLY, SELFISH SLAM-DANCE OF SNEERING, SNORTING, AND SNARLING!
OK, I'VE GIVEN YOU THE BENEFIT OF MY INSIGHT. NOW I'D LIKE TO SEE YOU DEAL WITH IT.

LIFE IN HELL
©1996 BY MATT GROENING
A WISE PHILOSOPHER ONCE SAID, "TO GET TO THE MOUNTAIN OF WISDOM, YOU HAVE TO TRAVEL THROUGH THE VALLEY OF STRUGGLE."
AND SAIL DOWN THE RIVER OF PETTY BICKERING.
AND LEAP OVER THE CANYON OF LINGERING RESENTMENTS.
AND WIND-SURF ACROSS THE LAKE OF ENDLESS WHINING.
AND CLIMB THE CLIFFS OF SARCASTIC RETORTS.
AND DODGE THE BOULDERS OF SPITEFUL NEEDLING.
AND SWIM YOUR WAY OUT OF THE WHIRLPOOL OF NAGGING, NAGGING, NAGGING.
AND RUN SCREAMING THROUGH THE TUNNEL OF INSANE RELATIVES.
AND SLOG THROUGH THE SWAMP OF DESPERATE CLINGING.
AND SLIDE ACROSS THE ICE FLOES OF FROSTY SILENCE.
AND HACK THROUGH THE JUNGLES OF TALKING ABOUT THE RELATIONSHIP AT 2 A.M.
AND CROSS THE ROPE-BRIDGE OF MUTTERING BITTERLY UNDER ONE'S BREATH.
AND SCRAMBLE THROUGH THE FOREST OF PSYCHOTIC SCREECHING.
UNTIL YOU REACH YOUR FINAL DESTINATION: EMOTIONAL EXHAUSTIONVILLE.
I'VE GOT A CRAZY IDEA: LET'S TAKE SEPARATE VACATIONS THIS YEAR.

LIFE IN HELL
©1995 BY MATT GROENING
I GOT A JOB TODAY. I'M GOING TO BE AN EXOTIC DANCER.
YOU?
BWA HA HA HA HA HA HA HA HA HA HA HA HA HA HA HA HA HA HA HA
HYA HA HA HA HA HA HA HA HA HA HA HA HA HA HA HA HA HA HA HA
MWA HA HA HA HA HA HA HA HA HA HA HA HA HA HA HA HA HA HA HA
GYA HA HA HA HA HA HA HA HA HA HA HA HA HA HA HA HA HA
HWA HA HA HA
THEY'RE STILL HIRING.

LIFE IN HELL
©1994 BY MATT GROENING
RACE YOU FOR THE ICE CREAM?
WOO HOO!
SORRY, I ALREADY ATE ALL THE ICE CREAM. BUT IT IS NICE TO SEE YOU GET SOME EXERCISE.

LIFE IN HELL

©1991 BY MATT GROENING

OPENING BY INVITATION ONLY
IF WE LIVED IN A SMALL TOWN WE WOULDN'T HAVE CULTURAL OPPORTUNITIES LIKE THIS.

LIFE IN HELL

©1990 BY MATT GROENING

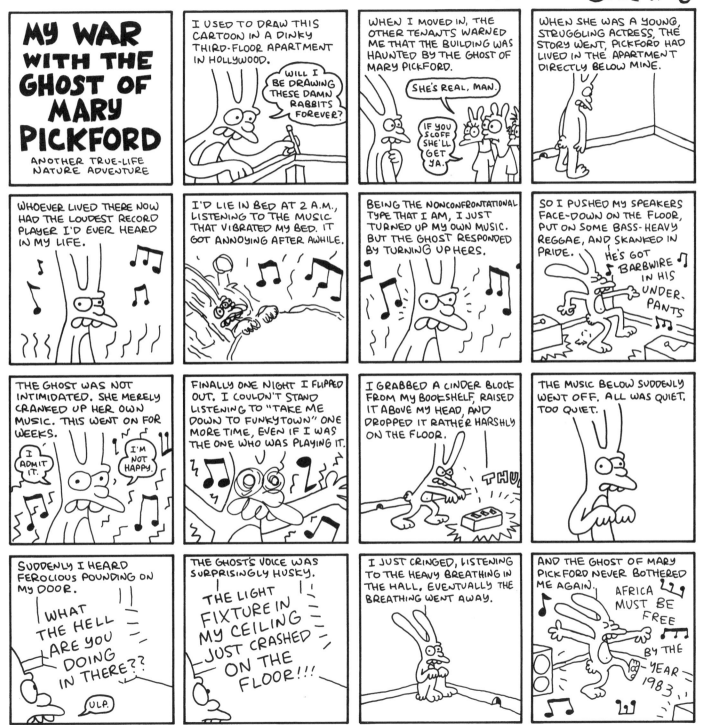

131

LIFE IN HELL

HEY... THIS ISN'T THE CORRECT WAY TO PLAY "TWISTER."

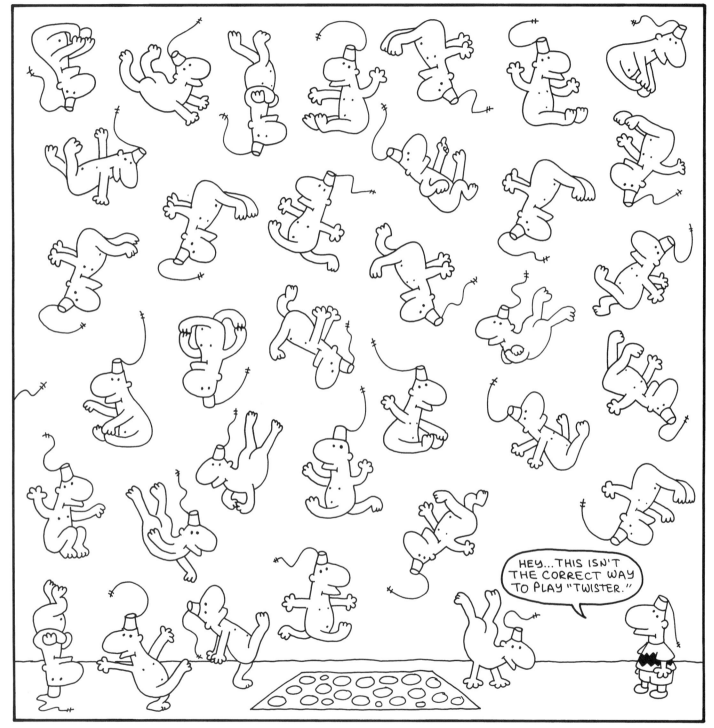

LIFE IN HELL
©1996 BY MATT GROENING
I GOTTA TELL YA, MAN: SOMETIMES YOUR INTENSE MOOD SWINGS ARE A BIT HARD TO HANDLE.
WHAT MOOD SWINGS?
WELL, ONE MOMENT YOU'RE FEELING BORED AND EMPTY...
YAWN SIGH.
THEN THE NEXT SECOND YOU SLIP INTO A STATE OF NERVOUS ANXIETY...
OH MY GOD, THIS ISN'T HAPPENING!
AND THEN COMES THE INEVITABLE OUTBURST OF ANGER.
THAT'S BECAUSE I HATE YOUR GUTS, YOU MISERABLE WORM!
THIS IS COMBINED WITH A PATTERN OF IMPULSIVE SELF-DESTRUCTIVENESS, OCCASIONALLY TAKING THE FORM OF ACTUAL SELF-MUTILATION.
BY THE WAY, YOU'LL NEVER GUESS WHAT I'M GOING TO HAVE PIERCED NEXT!
BECAUSE OF YOUR CONFUSED SENSE OF SELF, YOU CLING DESPERATELY IN ORDER TO AVOID FEELINGS OF TOTAL ABANDONMENT.
DON'T LEAVE ME! PLEASE!! I BEG YOU!
AND YOUR THINKING IS ALL-OR-NOTHING. YOU SEE PEOPLE AS EITHER ALL GOOD...
MY HERO!
OR ALL BAD.
YOU WORTHLESS BUM!!!
YOU SHIFT FROM COMPLETE IDEALIZATION...
MY SWEET, SWEET ANGEL.
TO EXPLOSIONS OF BITTERNESS AND RAGE.
THAT'S BECAUSE IT'S ALL YOUR FAULT FOR PROVOKING ME, YOU TWISTED FREAK!
DON'T YOU SEE? THAT'S EXACTLY WHAT I'M TALKING ABOUT! OH, IF ONLY YOU COULD TAKE RESPONSIBILITY FOR YOUR OWN BEHAVIOR!
OH WOW, YOU'RE RIGHT! I JUST HAD A FLASH OF INSIGHT, AND I REALIZE I'VE BEEN BEHAVING TERRIBLY. THANK YOU FOR POINTING ALL THIS STUFF OUT TO ME!
I VOW TO KEEP EXAMINING THE CAUSES OF MY OUTBURSTS AND I WANT YOU TO KNOW THAT I PROMISE, FROM THE BOTTOM OF MY HEART, TO ACT OUT OF LOVE RATHER THAN MISGUIDED ANGER.
IT MAKES ME FEEL SO MUCH BETTER TO HEAR THAT. PUTTING THOSE WILD MOOD SWINGS BEHIND US CAN ONLY ENHANCE OUR LOVE.
WHAT MOOD SWINGS?

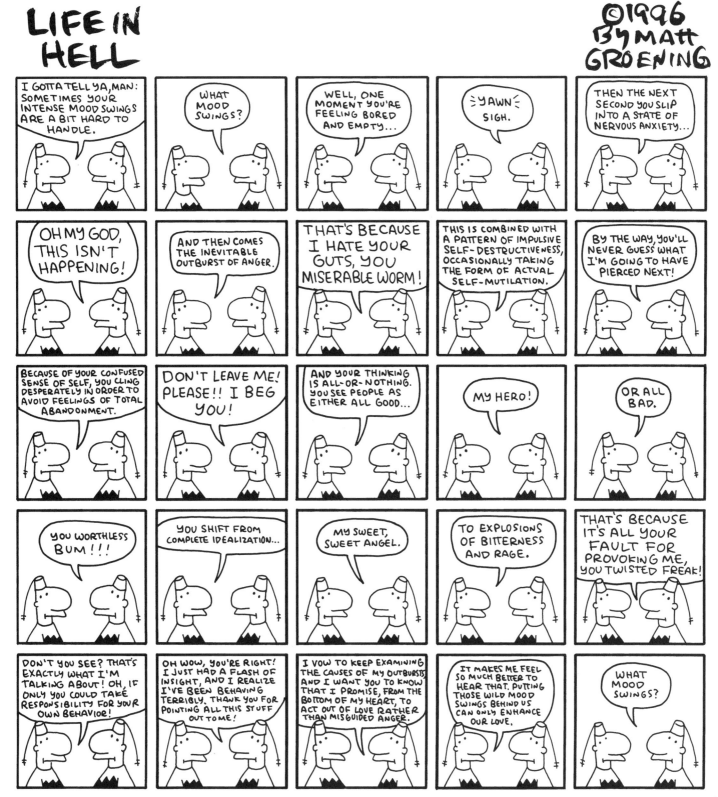

LIFE IN HELL

HAPPY NEW YEAR 1993
IF I WEREN'T SUCH A PEOPLE PERSON I'D BE TEMPTED TO KILL EVERYONE HERE TONIGHT.

LIFE IN HELL

©1991 BY MATT GROENING

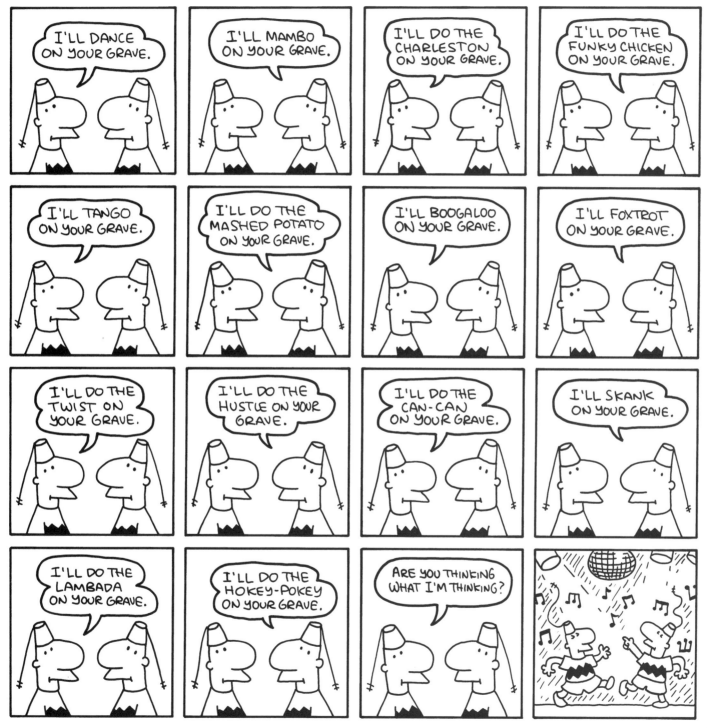

LIFE IN HELL
©1995 BY MATT GROENING
RACE YOU FOR THE ICE CREAM AGAIN?
YEE HAW!
BANG!
ONCE AGAIN, I ALREADY ATE ALL THE ICE CREAM. HOW MANY TIMES ARE YOU GOING TO KEEP FALLING FOR THIS TRICK?

LIFE IN HELL
© 1986 BY MATT GROENING
HELL FOR BEGINNERS
A BRIEF INTRODUCTION TO THIS CARTOON FOR NEOPHYTES AND A REMEDIAL COURSE FOR THOSE WHO HAVEN'T BEEN PAYING ATTENTION
WHAT IS "LIFE IN HELL"?
"LIFE IN HELL" IS A CUTE LITTLE COMIC STRIP FULL OF FUN, MERRIMENT, LAUGHS, AND FRIVOLITY.
NOT TO MENTION ANGST, ALIENATION, SELF-LOATHING, AND THE MEANINGLESSNESS OF OUR IMPENDING DOOM.
WHAT ARE THE MAJOR THEMES OF THIS CARTOON?
LOVE, SEX, WORK, DEATH, AND RABBITS.
WILL "LIFE IN HELL" OFFEND ME?
WE'LL DO
OUR BEST
WANNA PLAY LEAP FROG?
OK.
INTRODUCING...
NAME'S BINKY.
WOULD YOU MIND NOT STARING AT MY EARS?
WHO: STAR OF THIS CARTOON.
DISTINGUISHING FEATURES: TWO GROTESQUE EARS, BULGY EYES, CONSTANT TWITCHING.
EMOTIONAL STATE: BITTER, DEPRESSED, NORMAL.
HIS ESTRANGED GIRLFRIEND...
SHEBA HERE.
I'M PREMENSTRUAL AT THE MOMENT.
WHO: RABBIT ON-THE-GO.
DISTINGUISHING FEATURES: BASICALLY, BINKY IN DRAG.
EMOTIONAL STATE: GENERALLY MIFFED, OCCASIONALLY STEAMED.
THOSE TWO LITTLE FUN GUYS...
HE'S AKBAR.
HE'S JEFF.
WE'RE AKBAR AND JEFF.
WHO: BROTHERS, OR LOVERS, OR BOTH.
DISTINGUISHING FEATURES: FEZZES, BOTH EYES ON SAME SIDE OF HEAD.
EMOTIONAL STATE: INSCRUTABLE.
BINKY'S ILLEGITIMATE SON...
I'M BONGO.
PLEASE QUIT STARING AT MY EAR, PLEASE.
WHO: NO ONE REALLY CARES.
DISTINGUISHING FEATURES: TAKE A GUESS.
EMOTIONAL STATE: SQUELCHED.
WILL THE CHARACTERS IN "LIFE IN HELL" EVER ACHIEVE HAPPINESS?
WHAT A SILLY QUESTION! BINKY AND THE GANG WILL BE AS HAPPY AS YOU ARE.

LIFE IN HELL

CHEAPEST LOGO YET

R U EASILY PROVOKED?

©1982 BY MATT ~~GROENNING~~ ~~GROENTNIN~~ GROENING GODDAMMIT

I'M TALKING TO **YOU**, GOOFUS.

DO LITTLE THINGS TICK YOU OFF? DO PETTY FRUSTRATIONS BUG YOU? DO MINOR ANNOYANCES DRIVE YOU UP THE WALL? DO REPETITIOUS LITTLE QUESTIONS THAT INSULT YOUR INTELLIGENCE AND WASTE YOUR VALUABLE TIME REALLY REALLY REALLY JUST PISS YOU OFF? I THOUGHT SO.

HELL, NUTHIN' BOTHERS ME.
I'M NOT FAZED BY ANYTHING.
YOU DO YER THANG AN I'LL DO MINE.
A SUNNY DISPOSISH WILL ALWAYS SEE YOU THROUGH.
YOU BETCHA.
LET'S HAVE LUNCH SOON.

WE LIVE IN DANGEROUS TIMES, FULL OF CHILDISH PRANKS, SENSELESS CHATTER, AND FOOLISH HORSEPLAY. "CHEER UP," "JOIN THE PARTY," AND "WHAT'S COOKIN', GOOD-LOOKIN'?" ARE BUT A FEW OF THE IRRITATING PHRASES THAT TODAY'S GOOD-TIME CHARLIES AND CHARLEENAS CHORTLE HEARTILY, EGGING US SENSIBLE TYPES TO "RELAX," "HAVE FUN," AND "LET DOWN YOUR BARRIERS"— KNOWING FULL WELL THAT WE'D RATHER SEETHE IN SELF-CONSCIOUS SILENCE FOR OUR ENTIRE LIVES. WHAT'S THEIR PROBLEM? ARE THEY TRYING TO PROVOKE US?

UNFORTUNATELY, YES. THAT'S HOW THEY GET THEIR PERVERTED LITTLE THRILLS. AND THAT'S WHY WE MUST NEVER SUCCUMB TO THEIR SLY TRICKERY AND INSIDIOUS MIRTH. WE MUST REMAIN CALM AT ALL TIMES. NEVER LET THEM GET TO US NO MATTER WHAT. WE MUST SAVE FACE, MAINTAIN DIGNITY, AND KEEP OUR CHINS UP. IT WON'T BE EASY, AND IT CERTAINLY WON'T BE FUN--THAT'S ONE CONSOLATION--BUT THE JOB IS THERE SO SCRUB UP AND DIG IN. WE HAVE NOTHING TO FEAR BUT CHEER ITSELF. NOW GET OUT THERE AND KICK SOME ASS. AND BEWARE OF GUSTO.

THEY'LL TRY TO PROVOKE YOU AT WORK

IN TRAFFIC

EVEN AT HOME

HOW'S IT HANGIN', BINKLES?
GODDAMNED DUCKS.
QUEK
QUIK
QUOK
QUOKE
QUAKE
HEL-LO?
IS PORKY THERE?
NO. YOU MUST HAVE THE WRONG PHONE NUMBER.
NO--I MUST HAVE THE WRONG PIG.

REMEMBER, PROVOCATEURS ARE EVERYWHERE, SO TREAD LIGHTLY AND CARRY A BIG MUDDY STICK. THIS MESSAGE HAS BEEN PRINTED EXTRA-TINY SO YOU HAVE TO SQUINT WHILE READING IT--SQUINTING MAKES YOU LOOK UNCOMFORTABLE AND UNFRIENDLY AND IS THEREFORE DESIRABLE.

IF YOU FIND YOURSELF IN A SITUATION THAT YOU CAN'T CONTAIN, TRY COUNTING TO TEN BEFORE YOU BLOW UP.

1
2
3
4
5
6
7
8
9

LIFE IN HELL
©1996 BY MATT GROENING
HI, HONEY, I'M-- ULP!
I FIND THIS VERY UPSETTING.
I COME HOME FROM A HARD DAY AT WORK AND YOU'RE CAVORTING NAKEDLY.
I'M MISERABLE AND YOU'RE HAPPY.
THE WHOLE WORLD IS MISERABLE AND YOU'RE HAPPY.
YOU NEVER CHANGE THE CAT BOX.
THERE'S WAR AND FAMINE AND DISEASE, YOU KNOW.
YOU ALWAYS HOG THE REMOTE CONTROL.
AND WHAT ABOUT OPPRESSION?
YOU NEVER SEND ME FLOWERS.
YOU ALWAYS TAKE THE FLUFFY PILLOW.
PEOPLE ARE STARVING, YOU KNOW.
I NOW REALIZE WHAT A SELFISH, SHALLOW PERSON YOU ARE.
YOU SICKEN ME.
CARE TO DANCE?
I THOUGHT YOU'D NEVER ASK.

CLIP AND SAVE
LIFE IN HELL
FUN PAGE
TO BE READ UNDER THE COVERS LATE AT NIGHT WITH A CHEAP FLASHLIGHT AND A BOWL OF CHOCOLATE ICE CREAM
WHICH RABBIT IS THE HALLUCINATION?
OVER THERE!
NO, OVER THERE!
HOW TO DRAW COMICS THE LIFE IN HELL WAY
LEARN HOW TO DRAW ONE CHARACTER WELL. IT MAY TAKE AN ENTIRE SCHOOL CAREER OF ENDLESS DOODLING, BUT UPON GRADUATION YOU WILL HAVE A MEAL TICKET FOR LIFE.
VARY THE EXPRESSIONS AND MOVEMENTS OF YOUR CHARACTER ONLY SLIGHTLY EACH FRAME. MODERN, JADED READERS, NUMBED BY GARISH MEDIA VIOLENCE, WILL COME TO APPRECIATE THE SUBTLE VISUAL VARIATIONS.
BE CAREFUL, HOWEVER, IF YOU STRAY FROM THE STANDARD GAG FORMAT. SOME FOLKS DON'T UNDERSTAND WHEN ANTHROPOMORPHIC CARTOON CHARACTERS DEVIATE FROM THE TRADITIONAL SET-UP AND PAY-OFF COMIC-STRIP FORMULA, SO BE PREPARED IF YOU EXPERIMENT. AND REMEMBER: IF YOU DRAW YOURSELF INTO A CORNER, JUST HAVE YOUR CHARACTER COVER ITS FACE IN EMBARRASSMENT.
SOMETHING LIKE THIS.
RIDDLE TIME!
1. WHAT GENDER IS THE RABBIT?
2. WHERE CAN THE RABBIT GET A DECENT, AFFORDABLE APARTMENT IN TOWN?
3. IF GOD IS OMNIPOTENT, GOOD, AND JUST, WHY IS THERE SO MUCH MISERY AND SUFFERING IN THE WORLD?
REPLY TO LIFE IN HELL, c/o THIS NEWSPAPER.
LIFE IN HELL MYSTERY SMELL
SCRATCH AND SNIFF
CLOSE YOUR EYES, SCRATCH THE SPECIALLY-COATED ODOR BAR, INHALE DEEPLY WITH BOTH NOSTRILS, THEN TAKE A GUESS. ANSWER BELOW.
ANSWER: A COMBINATION AROMA OF INK AND PROCESSED WOOD PULP.

HAPPILY EVER AFTER

HOW CAN YOU BE HAPPY WHEN YOU KNOW I'M BITTER AND DEPRESSED?

LIFE IN HELL
©1994 BY MATT GROENING
IMPORTANT QUESTIONS ABOUT CARTOONING
BY WILL
WHY DO YOU ALWAYS DRAW BUNNIES??
DO YOU GET PAID MONEY TO DRAW BUNNIES??
WHY DO YOU DRAW ME AS A BUNNY ALL THE TIME??
CAN'T YOU DRAW NOTHING ELSE BUT BUNNIES??
WHY DON'T YOU DRAW MONSTERS??
DO YOU HAVE A JOB??
DO YOU LOVE BUNNIES??
WHY CAN'T YOU DRAW SCARY MONSTERS??
DON'T YOU LOVE MONSTERS??
WHY DO YOUR MONSTERS LOOK LIKE BUNNIES??
COULD YOU DRAW DUCKS??
BUT WHY BUNNIES??
DO THE PEOPLE OF THE WORLD LOVE BUNNIES??
WHY DO THEY LOOK THAT WAY??
WHY DON'T YOUR BUNNIES EVEN LOOK LIKE BUNNIES???

LIFE IN HELL
©1994 BY MATT GROENING
MOVIES I'M GOING TO MAKE WHEN I GROW UP
BY WILL
THE ZOMBOID WALKS UPON EARTH
THERE'S A DRAGON BEHIND YOUR CLOSET
COFFIN OF THE MUMMY
THE INVISIBLE CREATURE AND THE GOLDEN CRYSTAL
THE SCARY BUTCHER
SON OF THEM
BEWARE OF THE KILLER CRAB
I MARRIED A CYCLOPS (BECAUSE NO MAN EXISTED)
DOUBLE HEAD IN THE HIDDEN DOOR
THE AGE OF THE MONSTER
THE BEHEMOTH MEETS THE TERROR OF THE KILLER COBRA
ZOMBIES RULE THE END OF THE WORLD
TWO MONSTERS ISLAND
THE KILLER CATS MEET THE SUCKIN' DEAD
MY FATHER IS A BLACK CAT
MY BROTHER IS A SCORPION VAMPIRE
PINK-ZILLA
THE TONGUE CHOMPER
SLIME BORK
WELL, YOU ARE DEAD
MY PRESIDENT IS A DEMON
THE RAT IS HIDING IN THE SEWERS
MY MOTHER IS A SQUID BEAST
SPACE ALIENS LAND ON THE FARM
THE EARTH SHATTERS
THE GIRL IS A SHE-DEVIL
THE GHOST IS BEHIND YOU
WRECK OF THE SLUG
THE SKULL AND THE WEREWOLF
TERROR BUNNIES MEET THE KILLER FLASHLIGHT
THE TARANTULA FIGHTS THE TENTACLE
THE SEA ZOMBIES VS. THE SHARK
THE GOBLIN WITH THE GIRL HEAD
THE ENORMOUS MAN MEETS THE SLUG
SUCKERS OF LIGHTNING BENEATH THE EARTH
THE SHARK AND THE GIRL SPACE ALIENS
THE DEMON COST A LIFE
THE FOUR ZOMBIES ARE A MONSTER
I MARRIED A BITING WITCH (I MADE THIS UP WHEN I WAS FOUR)
THE TWO-TONGUE FROG
THE DAD, THE DUCK, AND THE DEMON
DON'T GO IN THAT CAVE
HALF-FLY, HALF-GIRL
YOU CAN'T KILL A ZOMBIE
SPOOKY TALES THAT WILL MAKE YOU SHRIEK
I GOING TO MAKE A MOVIE TOO: ZOMBIES ARE FOR REAL!
NO YOU AREN'T.

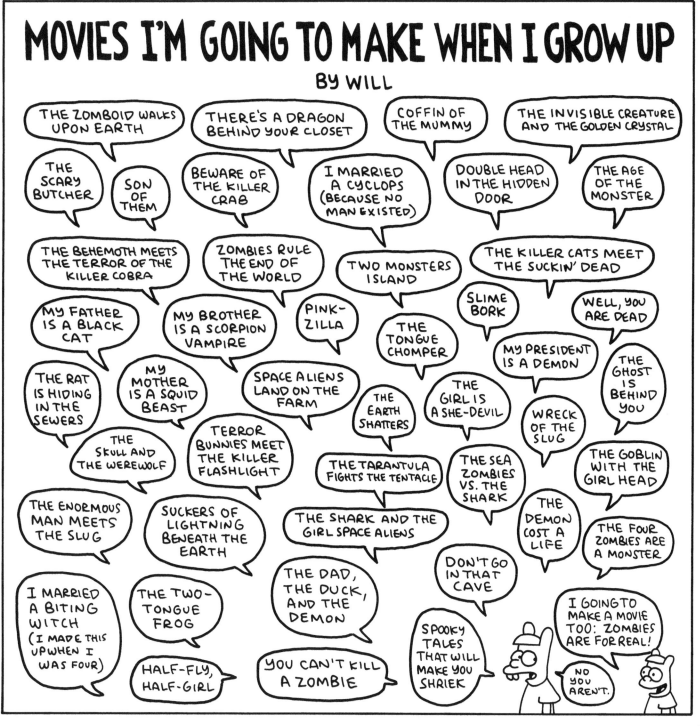

LIFE IN HELL
©1994 BY MATT GROENING
WOW! I JUST WATCHED THE NIXON FUNERAL ON TV.
I HAD NO IDEA HE WAS SUCH A GREAT STATESMAN, MAN.
WHAT THE HELL ARE YOU TALKING ABOUT?
NIXON WAS A LYING, EVIL SLEAZEBALL FOR HIS ENTIRE LIFE.
EVERYTHING NIXON DID WAS SHROUDED IN LIES AND DECEIT. HE WOULD HAVE GONE TO JAIL, BUT HE WEASELED OUT OF IT BY HAVING HIS APPOINTED SUCCESSOR PARDON HIM.
NIXON NEEDLESSLY KEPT THE VIETNAM WAR GOING FOR YEARS, POINTLESSLY KILLING THOUSANDS OF AMERICANS AND VIETNAMESE.
NIXON WAS RESPONSIBLE FOR DROPPING MORE BOMBS ON VIETNAM THAN WERE USED IN ALL OF WORLD WAR II.
HE AND HIS WAR-CRIMINAL PAL KISSINGER WERE SO HEARTLESS THEY BOMBED NORTH VIETNAM ON CHRISTMAS.
NIXON CHEATED ON HIS TAXES, AND HIS VICE-PRESIDENT HAD TO RESIGN BECAUSE OF THE BRIBES HE TOOK.
NIXON SPENT HIS ENTIRE POLITICAL CAREER TRYING TO SMEAR HIS OPPONENTS, SUBVERT THE RIGHTS OF CITIZENS, AND SPY ON HIS "ENEMIES."
HE WAS A JOYLESS, ARROGANT PRIG WHO WAS GRIPPED BY RESENTMENT AND PARANOIA.
AND LET'S NOT FORGET THAT LITTLE MATTER OF THE WATERGATE SCANDAL.
NIXON HAD TO RESIGN AS THE MOST DISGRACED PRESIDENT IN AMERICAN HISTORY.
I'M JUST BAFFLED THAT NO ONE ON TV HAD THE GUTS TO SAY THE UNPLEASANT TRUTH.
AT YOUR FUNERAL, I'M GOING TO TELL EVERYONE YOU WERE REALLY CRANKY.

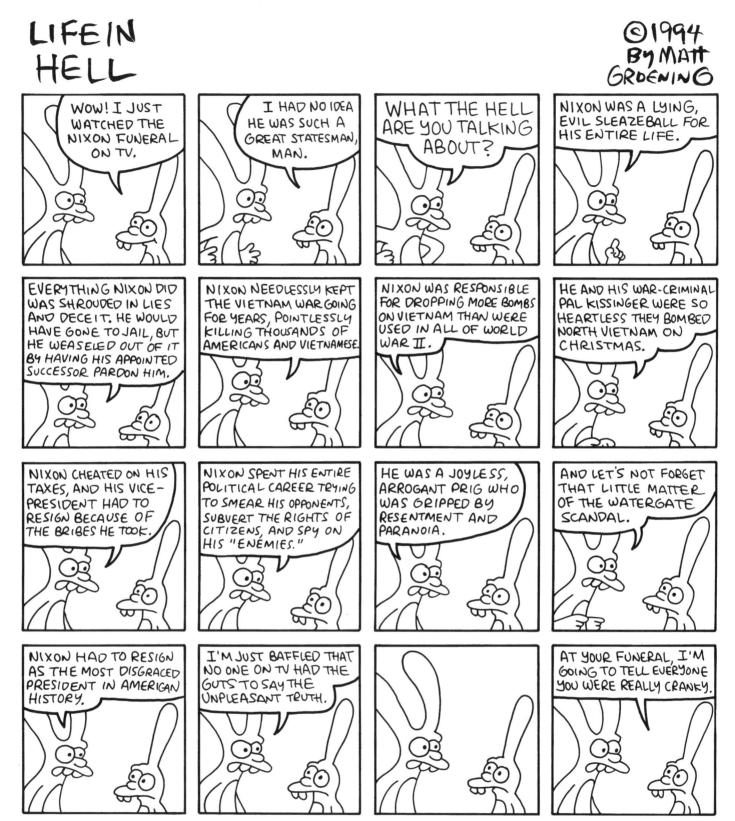

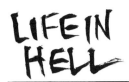

LIFE IN HELL

©1994 BY MATT GROENING

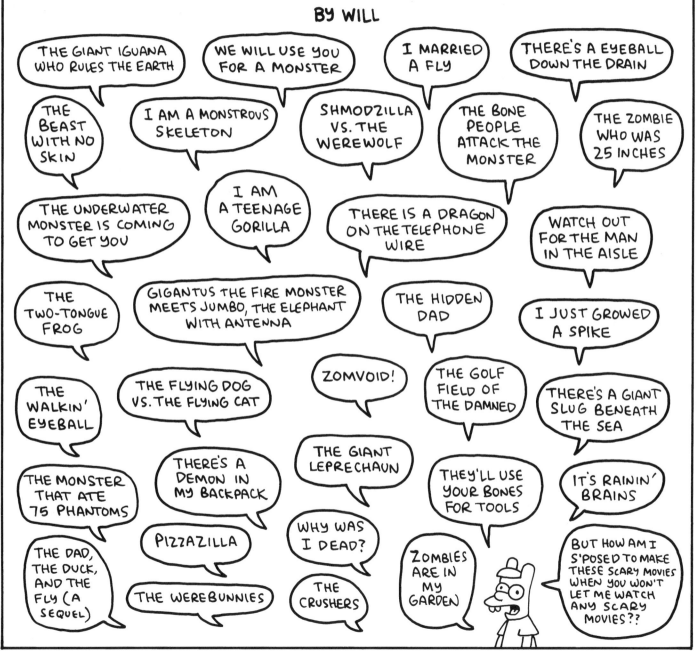

145

LIFE IN HELL
©1996 BY MATT GROENING
WANNA PLAY "EVIL MIND GAMES"?
HOW DO YOU PLAY?
THERE ARE NO RULES. YOU JUST TRY TO MANIPULATE YOUR OPPONENT WITH CUNNING AND DECEIT. THE WINNER IS THE PERSON WHO DRIVES THE OTHER PLAYER CRAZY.
YUCK! THAT SOUNDS TERRIBLE! I DON'T WANT TO PLAY ANY-THING SICK LIKE THAT.
IT'S KINDA FUN.
FUN? I REALLY THINK YOU SHOULD EXAMINE YOUR MOTIVES HERE. I'M ON TO YOU. YOU'RE NOT AS INNOCENT AS YOU MAKE YOURSELF OUT TO BE.
HEY, IT'S JUST A GAME.
YEAH, A GAME CALLED "EVIL MIND GAMES." SOME GAME!
OH, IT'S JUST A JOKE. LIGHTEN UP.
LOOK, I'M NOT GOING TO LET YOU OFF THE HOOK THAT EASILY. WHEN YOU PULL A STUPID STUNT LIKE THIS, PEOPLE'S FEELINGS GET HURT.
OKAY, OKAY. I'M SORRY I BROUGHT IT UP.
THAT DOESN'T EXCUSE IT. YOUR SO-CALLED HUMOR IS JUST A MASK FOR YOUR DEEP HOSTILITY.
I SAID I'M SORRY. WHAT MORE DO YOU WANT?
I WANT YOU TO TAKE RESPONSIBILITY FOR YOUR PASSIVE-AGGRESSIVE BEHAVIOR, AND PROMISE ME YOU'LL NEVER DO IT AGAIN.
I ADMIT MY "EVIL MIND GAMES" WAS A BAD IDEA, AND I PROMISE I'LL NEVER DO IT AGAIN.
I WIN!!!

LIFE IN HELL

© 1990 BY MATT GROENING

YOUR WORKING-DAY EMOTION CHECKLIST

LIFE IN HELL
©1994 BY MATT GROENING
THE NEW PLEDGE
I pledge allegiance to the flag
Against Anything Un- n
of the United States ~~of~~ America,
ans
and to the Republic for which it stands,
two s Jesus
~~one~~ nation, under ~~God~~,
rich against poor
~~Indivisible~~,
curtailed
with liberty and justice for all,
except blacks, homosexuals, women who want abortions, Communists, welfare queens, treehuggers, feminazis, illegal immigrants, children of illegal immigrants, and you if you don't watch your step.

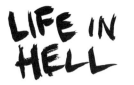
LIFE IN HELL

©1996 BY MATT GROENING

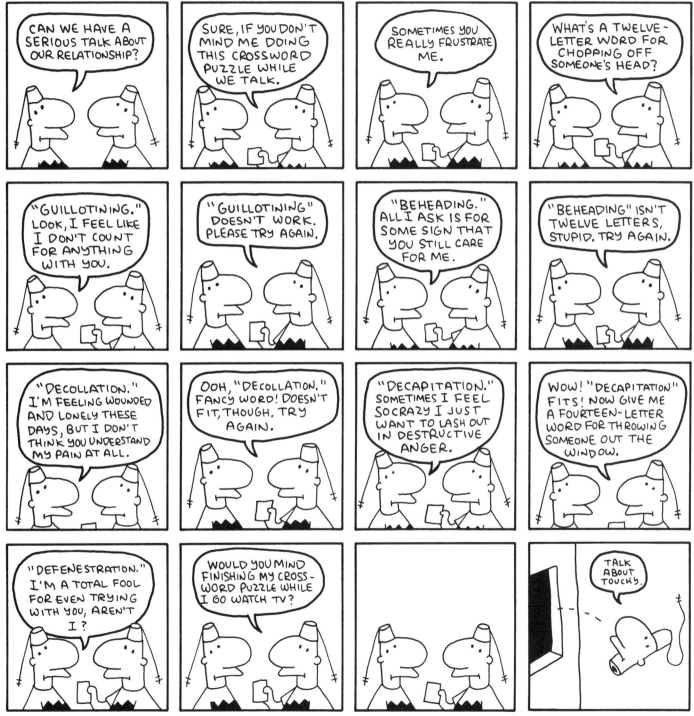

CAN WE HAVE A SERIOUS TALK ABOUT OUR RELATIONSHIP?

SURE, IF YOU DON'T MIND ME DOING THIS CROSSWORD PUZZLE WHILE WE TALK.

SOMETIMES YOU REALLY FRUSTRATE ME.

WHAT'S A TWELVE-LETTER WORD FOR CHOPPING OFF SOMEONE'S HEAD?

"GUILLOTINING." LOOK, I FEEL LIKE I DON'T COUNT FOR ANYTHING WITH YOU.

"GUILLOTINING" DOESN'T WORK. PLEASE TRY AGAIN.

"BEHEADING." ALL I ASK IS FOR SOME SIGN THAT YOU STILL CARE FOR ME.

"BEHEADING" ISN'T TWELVE LETTERS, STUPID. TRY AGAIN.

"DECOLLATION." I'M FEELING WOUNDED AND LONELY THESE DAYS, BUT I DON'T THINK YOU UNDERSTAND MY PAIN AT ALL.

OOH, "DECOLLATION." FANCY WORD! DOESN'T FIT, THOUGH. TRY AGAIN.

"DECAPITATION." SOMETIMES I FEEL SO CRAZY I JUST WANT TO LASH OUT IN DESTRUCTIVE ANGER.

WOW! "DECAPITATION" FITS! NOW GIVE ME A FOURTEEN-LETTER WORD FOR THROWING SOMEONE OUT THE WINDOW.

"DEFENESTRATION." I'M A TOTAL FOOL FOR EVEN TRYING WITH YOU, AREN'T I?

WOULD YOU MIND FINISHING MY CROSSWORD PUZZLE WHILE I GO WATCH TV?

TALK ABOUT TOUCHY.

149

LIFE IN HELL

©1990
BY MATT
GROENING

HOW TO DRAW AKBAR & JEFF

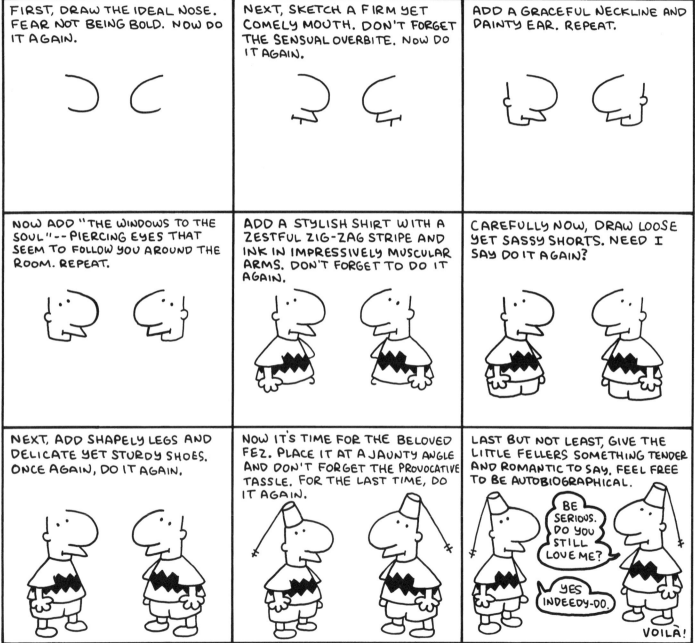

LIFE IN HELL
©1996 BY MATT GROENING
I FEEL LONELY.
I FEEL LONELY AND ISOLATED.
I FEEL LONELY AND ISOLATED AND BEREFT.
I FEEL LONELY AND ISOLATED AND BEREFT AND FORLORN.
I FEEL LONELY AND ISOLATED AND BEREFT AND FORLORN AND DESPONDENT.
I FEEL LONELY AND ISOLATED AND BEREFT AND FORLORN AND DESPONDENT AND DEPRESSED.
I FEEL LONELY AND ISOLATED AND BEREFT AND FORLORN AND DESPONDENT AND DEPRESSED AND ABANDONED.
I FEEL LONELY AND ISOLATED AND BEREFT AND FORLORN AND DESPONDENT AND DEPRESSED AND ABANDONED AND DEJECTED.
I FEEL LONELY AND ISOLATED AND BEREFT AND FORLORN AND DESPONDENT AND DEPRESSED AND ABANDONED AND DEJECTED AND GLOOMY.
I FEEL LONELY AND ISOLATED AND BEREFT AND FORLORN AND DESPONDENT AND DEPRESSED AND ABANDONED AND DEJECTED AND GLOOMY AND HOPELESS.
I FEEL LONELY AND ISOLATED AND BEREFT AND FORLORN AND DESPONDENT AND DEPRESSED AND ABANDONED AND DEJECTED AND GLOOMY AND HOPELESS AND DISHEARTENED.
I FEEL LONELY AND ISOLATED AND BEREFT AND FORLORN AND DESPONDENT AND DEPRESSED AND ABANDONED AND DEJECTED AND GLOOMY AND HOPELESS AND DISHEARTENED AND WRETCHED.
I FEEL LONELY AND ISOLATED AND BEREFT AND FORLORN AND DESPONDENT AND DEPRESSED AND ABANDONED AND DEJECTED AND GLOOMY AND HOPELESS AND DISHEARTENED AND WRETCHED AND HELPLESS.
I FEEL LONELY AND ISOLATED AND BEREFT AND FORLORN AND DESPONDENT AND DEPRESSED AND ABANDONED AND DEJECTED AND GLOOMY AND HOPELESS AND DISHEARTENED AND WRETCHED AND HELPLESS AND INCONSOLABLE.
I FEEL LONELY AND ISOLATED AND BEREFT AND FORLORN AND DESPONDENT AND DEPRESSED AND ABANDONED AND DEJECTED AND GLOOMY AND HOPELESS AND DISHEARTENED AND WRETCHED AND HELPLESS AND INCONSOLABLE AND AROUSED.
I FEEL HAPPY.

LIFE IN HELL
©1996 BY MATT GROENING
I'VE DECIDED TO BECOME AN ARTIST.
WOW!
I'VE MADE A SYSTEMATIC STUDY OF ALL THE GREAT ARTISTS I ADMIRE, AND I'VE COMPILED A LIST OF THE THINGS THEY'VE DONE IN THE COURSE OF THEIR INCREDIBLY CREATIVE, AMBITIOUS CAREERS.
IT'S A SIMPLE MATTER OF GOING DOWN THE LIST, DOING WHAT THE GREAT ARTISTS DO!
BRILLIANT! HOW'S IT GOING SO FAR?
WELL, I'VE DEVELOPED AN ARTISTIC TEMPERAMENT.
I'M NOW PASSIONATE, REBELLIOUS, AND MOODY.
I HAVE A CONSTANT CRAVING FOR JACK DANIEL'S.
I'M GROWING A GOATEE.
I'VE GOT A TATTOO ON MY SHOULDER OF AN OBSCURE RELIGIOUS SYMBOL.
I GO TO ALL MY SO-CALLED FRIENDS' ART OPENINGS.
AT THESE OPENINGS I EAT AS MANY APPETIZERS AS I CAN CRAM IN MY MOUTH.
I'VE BECOME ADDICTED TO HEROIN.
I CALLED A GALLERY LAST WEEK AND THEY SAID TO CALL BACK NEXT WEEK.
I'VE BEEN FEELING VERY, VERY INSPIRED LATELY.
GREAT! I'D LIKE TO SEE YOUR WORK SOMETIME!
FIRST I NEED TO GET SOME ART SUPPLIES.

LIFE IN HELL

©1996 BY MATT GROENING

WILL & ABE'S GUIDE TO BALI
PART ONE
IF YOU LIKE TOADS, COME TO BALI!
THEY'RE FUN TO CATCH, TOO!
BALI IS AN ISLAND ON THE OTHER SIDE OF THE EARTH.
IT HAS VOLCANOES, TEMPLES, AND LOTS OF SWIMMING SNAKES!
THERE'S ALSO BIG COOL CATERPILLARS!
AND IF YOU HAVE A DAUGHTER, THERE'S LOTS OF BABY CHICKENS!
THEY HAVE REAL BIG TEMPLES HERE. THE TEMPLES IMITATE SPLIT-OPEN MOUNTAINS, WHICH MEANS HIGHER AND HIGHER TO HEAVEN.
YEAH!
THEY BELIEVE IN YIN AND YANG, AND THEY'RE VERY SERIOUS.
AND THE RICE THEY THROW UP IN THE AIR AND IT LANDS IN THE BASKET!
NO THEY DON'T.
SOMETIMES THEY DO.
NO!
I SAID, "SOMETIMES."
THAT ISN'T TRUE, FRIENDS. MY BROTHER'S WRONG.
NO, IT'S TRUE.
ABE!!!
DOWN BY THIS ONE TEMPLE THERE'S A CAVE WITH MORE THAN 6,000 OR MORE BATS.
MAYBE 60,000!
MAYBE 5 MILLION!
THE BAT POOP SMELLS BAD.
REALLY BAD.
OUR MOM ESPECIALLY COULDN'T STAND IT.
THEY DIDN'T WANT US TO GO IN THE BAT CAVE, BUT WE WENT IN ANYWAY. THE BABIES ARE CUTE, BUT BEWARE!
THERE'S HUGE RED AND ORANGE COCKROACHES IN THERE!
NEXT TIME WE'RE GOING TO TELL YOU ABOUT THE FOOD, THE ACTIVITIES, THE MONKEYS, AND THE CEREMONIES!
AND THIS WEIRD TOILET WE SAW IN THE RESTAURANT!

LIFE IN HELL
©1996 BY MATT GROENING
WILL & ABE'S GUIDE TO BALI
PART TWO
IF YOU COME TO BALI, REMEMBER IT'S GOING TO BE STRANGE AND DIFFERENT TO YOU.
IT'S A LOT DIFFERENT. THEY HAVE NO MAPLE SYRUP. THEY ONLY HAVE HONEY.
BALI IS A LONG TRIP TO GET HERE. FIRST YOU FLY TO HAWAII, THEN TO ANOTHER PLACE NEAR JAPAN, ANOTHER PLACE, ANOTHER PLACE, THEN ANOTHER PLACE BETWEEN JAPAN AND CHINA, THEN YOU LAND IN BALI.
IT TOOK MORE THAN TWO WHOLE TWO-HOUR MOVIES!
EVERYWHERE YOU GO YOU SEE RICE PADDIES SHAPED LIKE A STAIRCASE, AND WATER COMES THROUGH LITTLE HOLES TO MAKE WATERFALLS!
AND THERE'S A LOT OF RICE, TOO MUCH TO BE TRUE!
AT THE WEAVING VILLAGE, YOU CAN SEE A GIANT YAK!
WE ALSO SAW THESE REALLY COOL MONKEYS THERE. BUT WE COULDN'T TOUCH THEM OR PLAY WITH THEM BECAUSE THEY MIGHT HURT US REALLY BADLY.
THE MUSIC OF BALI HAS A NICE FAST BEAT. I WOULD DESCRIBE IT AS VERY FAST AND NOISY. THEY HAVE GONGS, SOME KIND OF BAMBOO DRUMS, AND A WOODEN FLUTE.
NOT A WOODEN FLUTE--A WOODEN FLUTE THINGY.
THEY HAVE LOTS OF STRANGE DANCES HERE! WE SAW THIS ONE WEIRD LADY WITH A BIG HAT WHO MOVES VERY FAST BUT STOPS STILL EVERY SECOND!
EVEN THOUGH IT WAS VERY LOUD, WE FELL ASLEEP UNDER THE STAGE!
THE DANCES ARE ABOUT REINDEERS, BUNNIES, NATURE, DEMONS, WOMEN HAVING RIGHTS, AND FROGS!
AND A LITTLE BIT OF YIN AND YANG!
AND NOW WE ARE IN A RESTAURANT AND WILL WON'T EAT HIS HAMBURGER!
THAT'S BECAUSE THE HAMBURGER TASTES DIFFERENT.

LIFE IN HELL

WILL & ABE'S GUIDE TO BALI
PART THREE
HI, DEMON!
BALI HAS LOTS OF GREAT MASKS AND DANCES AND VERY NICE STATUES OF DEMONS AND GHOULS!
THERE'S RANGDA THE WITCH. SHE'S A WOMAN WITCH.
EVERYBODY KNOWS THAT.
AND GARUDA IS A BIG BIRD.
VERY BIG.
AND BARONG LOOKS LIKE A BIG LION! HE'S A GOOD BEAST THAT FIGHTS RANGDA IN A NEVER-ENDING BATTLE! AND THERE'S THESE EVIL BLUE DEMON MONKEYS WITH BATWINGS THAT SERVE RANGDA!
IT'S LIKE THE WIZARD OF OZ, KIND OF.
YOU CAN GET MASKS AND WOODEN STATUES OF THESE AND OTHER MONKEY GODS AT THE MARKETPLACE!
BUT IF YOU GO THERE, GET READY FOR EVERYONE TO ASK YOU VERY BADLY TO BUY STUFF.
BE SURE TO TRY THIS REALLY COOL GAMBLING GAME AT THE MARKETPLACE! YOU THROW BALINESE MONEY ON CERTAIN PICTURES, AND THE OWNER OF THE GAME SHAKES UP THREE DICES IN A BOX! THE DICES HAVE PICTURES OF ANIMALS, LIKE SHARK, CRAB, EAGLE, HORSE! CRABS AND HORSES ARE LUCKY!
SHARKS ARE PRETTY LUCKY. BUT I SAY DON'T BET FOR THE CROCODILE!
IF YOU COME TO BALI, THERE ARE SOME RULES. YOU CAN'T POINT. YOU CAN'T DO ANYTHING WITH YOUR LEFT HAND. YOU AREN'T REALLY ALLOWED TO TOUCH PEOPLE'S HEADS.
YOU SHOULD NEVER EVER SHOW YOUR BARE FEET TO PEOPLE. AND NEVER PUT YOUR FEET ON THE TABLE. IT'S ANNOYING!
AND BE SURE TO BRING A FLASHLIGHT! YOU CAN SEE BATS AND BIG BULLFROGS! THERE'S ALSO LOTS OF RED ANTS WITH BIG MANDIBLES, AND WE KNOW THEIR QUEEN MUST BE DISGUSTING! DON'T SQUISH THEM, BECAUSE THEIR WHITE BLOOD STINGS YOU!
RED BLOOD!
WHITE!
RED!
THE BLOOD IS WHITE, OK FOLKS?
SO DON'T BE AFRAID! COME TO BALI! THE CHILDREN ARE FUN AND THE PEOPLE ARE VERY NICE!
THEY EVEN GIVE US CANDY!

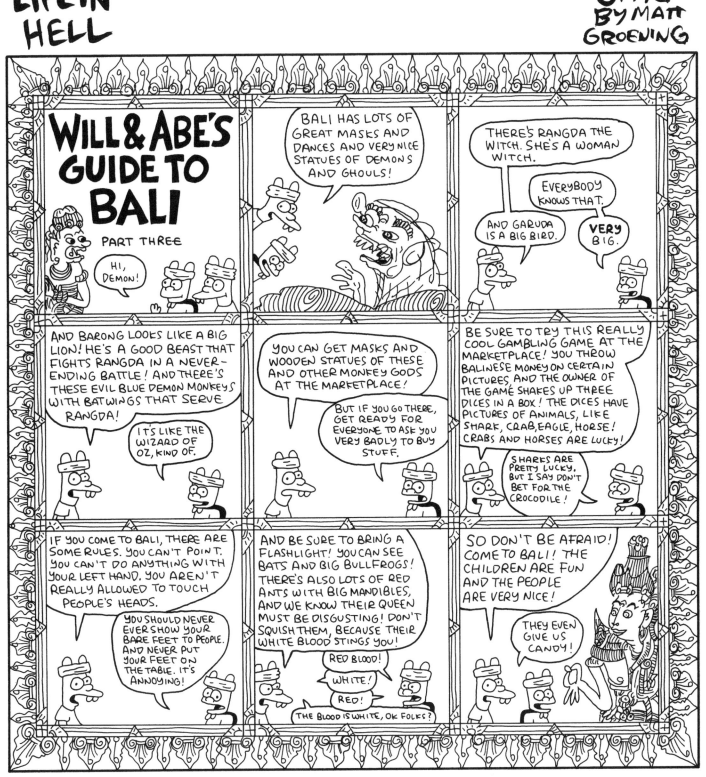

LIFE IN HELL
©1996 BY MATT GROENING
I'M SO HAPPY TODAY!
HOW CAN YOU BE HAPPY WHEN YOU KNOW I'M BITTER AND DEPRESSED?
I DON'T KNOW, BUT I'M REALLY HAPPY!
HOW CAN YOU BE HAPPY WHEN YOU KNOW I'M WRITHING IN THE AGONY OF MY OWN SELF-SABOTAGING BEHAVIOR?
ALL I CAN SAY IS I'M HAPPY!
HOW CAN YOU BE HAPPY WHEN YOU KNOW I HAVE SUCH LOW SELF-ESTEEM? ANSWER ME THAT.
I'M STILL HAPPY!
HOW CAN YOU BE HAPPY WHEN YOU KNOW I'M FULL OF NAMELESS FEARS AND IRRATIONAL ANXIETIES BORDERING ON THE DELUSIONAL?
I'M TRYING TO BE HAPPY!
HOW CAN YOU TRY TO BE HAPPY WHEN YOU KNOW I AM BESIEGED BY SELF-DOUBT AND EXISTENTIAL PANIC?
I GUESS I'M NOT SO HAPPY AFTER ALL.
HOW CAN YOU BE EVEN SEMI-HAPPY WHEN YOU YOU KNOW I'M VAGUELY DISSATISFIED WITH THE WAY MY LIFE HAS GONE SO FAR?
WHY MUST I BE UNHAPPY JUST BECAUSE YOU ARE UNHAPPY? ON THE CONTRARY, WHY CAN'T YOU BE HAPPY BECAUSE I AM HAPPY?
HOW CAN YOU SUGGEST I BE HAPPY LIKE YOU WHEN YOU KNOW YOU'RE REALLY UNHAPPY?
I GIVE UP.
I'M SO HAPPY TODAY!

LIFE IN HELL
©1996 BY MATT GROENING
HEY, WHAT HAPPENED TO YOUR INSPIRATIONAL PLAQUE?
JU ST DO IT.

ZZK
ZZK
ZZK

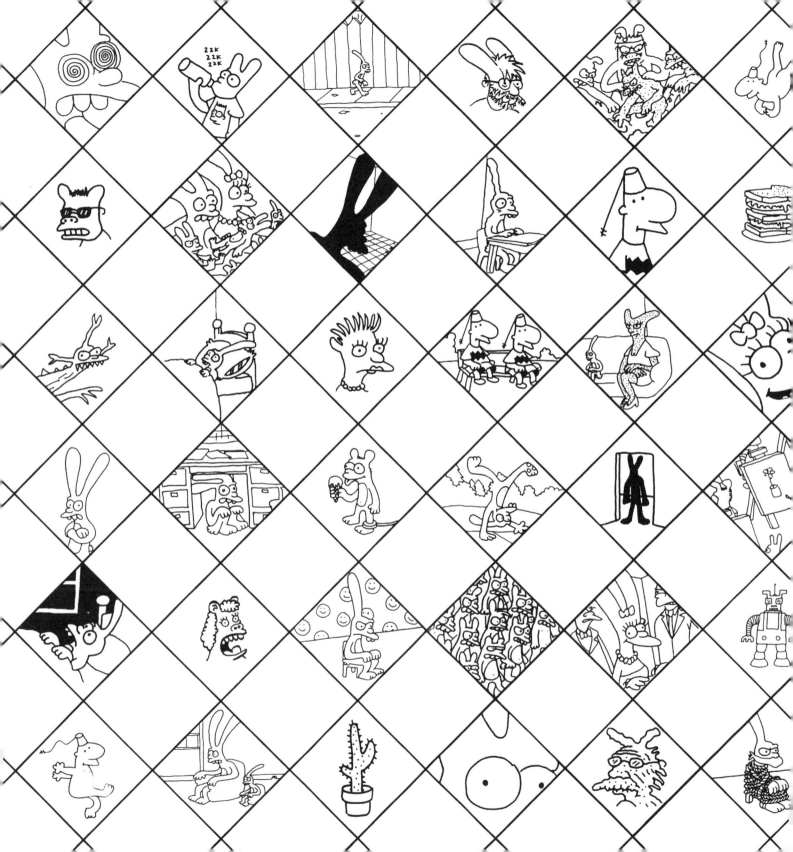

MAD

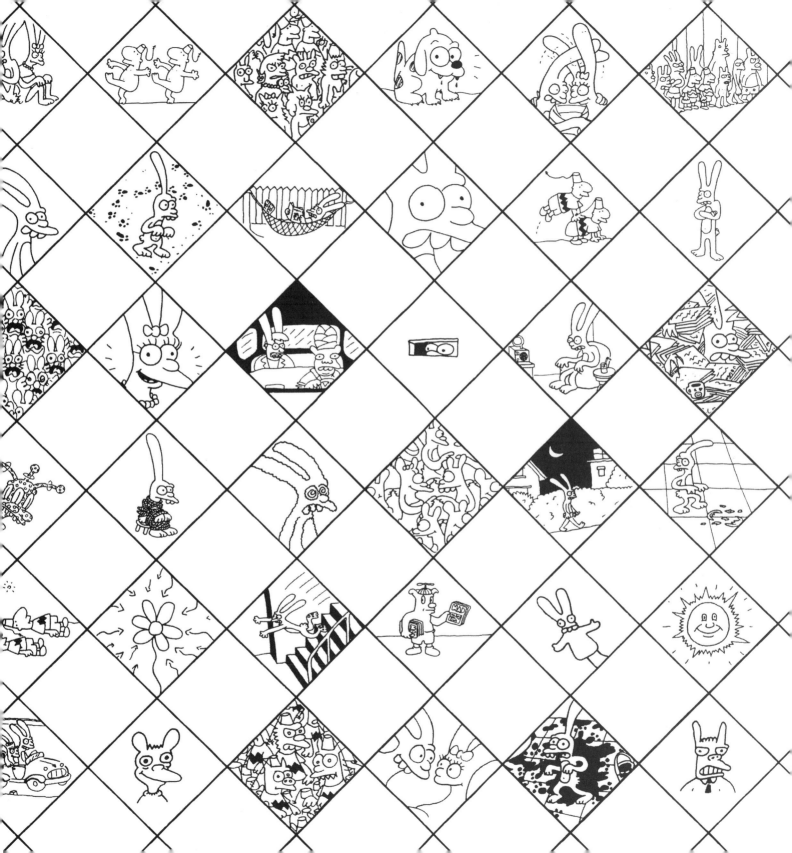